KIDS IN THE RIOT: HIGH AND LOW WITH THE LIBERTINES

PETE WELSH

OMNIBUS PRESS

London / New York / Paris / Sydney / Copenhagen / Madrid / Toky

D0228424

Exclusive Distributors
Music Sales Limited,
8/9 Frith Street,
London W1D 3JB, UK.

Music Sales Corporation,
257 Park Avenue South,
New York, NY 10010, USA.

Macmillan Distribution Services,
53 Park West Drive,
Derrimut, Vic 3030,
Australia.

To the Music Trade only:
Music Sales Limited,
8/9 Frith Street,
London W1D 3JB, UK.

Every effort has been made to trace the copyright holders of the photographs in this book but one or two were unreachable. We would be grateful if the photographers concerned would contact us.

Typeset by Galleon Typesetting, Ipswich.
Printed by Creative Print & Design, Ebbw Vale, Wales.

A catalogue record for this book is available from the British Library.

Visit Omnibus Press on the web at www.omnibuspress.com

CONTENTS

ACKNOWLEDGEMENTS

My brother Rob, Mum and Dad for endless encouragement, like-wise, Mick Whitnall and Steve Diggle. Mark, Cess, Tom, Jerry White. Terry Rawlings and Paul McEvoy, Alan Parker, Gary Crowley, Eddie Piller, Lisa, Rich and Stu, Amy, Cat and Emma, Afonso Pinto, Annalisa, Kerry, Linda & Amanda, Roger Sargent, Tony Linkin, James Endeacott, James Mullord, Chev, Chris Charlesworth, Andy Neill, Adrian Hunter, Alan McGee, Stephen King, Pete Jackson, Goati, Banny Poostchi, Billy and Ginger, Simon White, Chris Sullivan, Geoff Travis, Paul Hallam, Dean Fragile, Gary Loveridge, John Morris, Toby McFarlane, Ricky and Roy Shaft, Mark Collings, Pat Gilbert, Duffy and Mani, Graham Gillespie, Sym Gharial, Adam Evans, Steve Bedlow, Filthy McNasty's Whiskey Café, The Good Mixer, The Vetch Field.

Pete Welsh
London
October 2004

"*We decided to throw ourselves into eternity*"
— Carl Barat

"*He loves me but in the way that old sailors love each other*"
— Pete Doherty

FOREWORD

The Libertines story probably started the minute Peter met Carl but, in managing the band over the last 12 months, I soon learned it's more than a group, it's a belief system. The fans that follow The Libertines are like no other fans I have ever encountered – they are true fanatics. This book may well be the story of Peter and Carl but in reality it's about the story of The Libertines' fans because like all the truly great bands (The Who, the Pistols or The Clash) The Libertines are a mirror image of their fans with all the flaws and genius that make up people who are alive and have a go at trying to get out of their mundane existences.

By the end of the last decade the music business corporates had it all sewn up again. In times like this it will always come down to the musicians changing the rules. The Libertines, more than any other group since 1977, have done this, so the DIY revolution re-emerged. The culture they have inspired will be felt in 25 years time. They are that important to British culture. Whether they can hold it together, only time will tell but, musically, the chemistry between the four people in the group is undeniably brilliant.

This last year has been a rollercoaster for all the fans and anybody that has been personally involved. The most important band of their generation? By a country mile. The best live band in the world? Undeniably. It's all in The Libertines' hands from here on in, nobody else's. Their first two albums are up there with all the great records the critics rave on about, being great British rock'n'roll records on a par with any band. The great thing about great music is that it's always timeless. Here's hoping that just like the movies there's a happy ending for all involved.

Alan McGee
October 2004.

INTRODUCTION

For Pete's Sake

I SHOULD first forewarn you that this story will feature a freakishly excessive headcount of characters with the Christian name Pete. After yours truly there's of course Pete Doherty, then Pete Wolf, Peter Perrett, *little* Peter Perrett, Pete Voss, Rock Pete, Micro Pete, and little gay Pete. It's a cast of dozens and anyone called Pete in the area and timescale of these memoirs will testify that a prefix/suffix or nickname is/was a must.

Fittingly, my life with The Libertines started when this Pete met that Pete in the Camden Town dwelling of Micro Pete.

It was a Tuesday, sometime in 1997, after a night at the now defunct HQ club (don't look for it, it's not there any more), where the God-awful New Romantic revival Ro-Mo had its 15 minutes. The usual cast of misfits had gone back to Micro Pete's self-styled party-pad to drain the last dregs of the night. I was wrestling over a can of warm lager when I noticed a young kid I'd never seen before, cross-legged on the floor with an acoustic guitar, belting out a Chas'n'Dave number, with a chirrupy 'Parklife'-esque bonhomie. It was all well and good, but hey kid, Britpop's dead, right? Now, of course, this is the bit where I say I witnessed something special the moment I heard the first "rabbit, rabbit" – that I was party to the future of rock'n'roll. But I didn't.

I saw a peculiar kid playing Chas and fucking Dave and got a night bus home.

CHAPTER 1

London Calling

I WOULD see this kid who I now know as Pete Doherty intermittently over the next few years, slowly getting to know him better. To be honest, he was just another geezer going on about his band all the time and I didn't take anything more than a passing interest in what he was up to until I learned he was in league with another post-Britpop hopeful I knew very well. I'd had a band called The Samaritans and the first person I'd recruited was a young local bass player called John Hassall. I overlooked the fact that at 16 he was nearly 10 years my junior and got him involved because he had a Rickenbacker bass which he claimed had belonged to Jim Lea out of Slade. That and the fact that he played it well were all the credentials I needed.

John's obsession with The Beatles even put mine in the shade. If he wasn't listening to the Fabs he'd be belting out 'Blackbird' or 'I'm Looking Through You' on his acoustic. Another favourite on the Hassall household turntable, and one he probably won't want reminding of was 1988's 'Anfield Rap', a bizarre and cringe-inducing football song featuring the dubious vocal talents of John Barnes, which he'd sing along with word for word. His trusty Beatles were never far away though, and around this time, I opened his ears to the likes of The Clash and The Stranglers, which I like to think helped provide a grounding for his later role in the full-on punk rock assault of The Libertines. However, when John started professing an interest in morris dancing I had to concede that that was a musical genre I couldn't give him any guidance in.

For about a year we basically mucked about with guitars in the basement of his mum's house in Kentish Town. John's 18th birthday was approaching and myself and the others in the band were geeing him up about what he was going to do to celebrate. I could tell something was weighing heavily on the young chap's mind and after some probing he came clean that it wasn't his 18th but the significantly lesser milestone of turning 17. This meant that when I'd enlisted him for The Samaritans he was all of 15. Shit. "Was this legal," I thought? John explained he'd told me he was 16 as he thought I would have been prejudiced if he had told the truth. I wouldn't have, but still something wasn't quite right. We all liked the kid but in truth his face didn't really fit for that particular band. Maybe he *was* too young, maybe his playing style was a bit busy, and maybe I had someone waiting in the wings who would be more suitable.

Whatever, I told John he was out and I think he took it quite hard which, in turn, upset me. That said I was pretty sure that closing one door on him would open another. He had his own songs, and was prodigiously talented on his instrument. In fact, I remember remarking to the other guys, "What's the bet he'll have a record deal before any of us?" Though never in a million years would I have thought I'd one day be writing a book about his band. Being more focussed on music than having a good time, I knew John would succeed and sure enough he certainly had the last laugh.

The reason John would come back to haunt me and have that last laugh was that he too had met and become acquainted with that fresh-faced troubadour with a penchant for Chas'n'Dave, the nascent Pete Doherty. I was pleased for John as they were more the same age group, and along with another of their mates, Carl, they looked like a cool little gang. I still didn't take too much notice.

After all, I had scores of friends and acquaintances in bands struggling along like I was with varying degrees of progression, what was to set these kids apart as the "one's most likely"?

CARL: "The first time I laid eyes on Pete Doherty? I'd been good friends with his sister at drama school. She was my only ally in this world of [*snorts derisively*] students. I was expecting everyone to be like *Withnail And I* – passionate like I was – but I ended up in this halls of residence that was like a prison block with hockey sticks. I was gutted, heartbroken. I had nothing in common with any of these kids. The one person, the one saving grace was Pete's sister, Amy-Jo. We were friends, fucking *good* friends – nothing saucy, funnily enough. She kept telling me about this younger brother she had and that he was a poet. I was instantly jealous of him. I was jealous from the off, you know, some bird's brother. You don't want another male influence on a bird, do you?

"So one day she says he's coming up. Turns out he's as intrigued to meet me as I am him. He's meant to be intelligent too. Prior to us meeting he sends me a letter in the post asking if I can tab 'This Charming Man' by The Smiths. I can't fucking stand The Smiths, worse still I think he means 'Charmless Man' by Blur which is even worse, so I think no fucking *way*.

"Then he turns up to the halls and Amy goes, 'My brother's here but I've got to go to night class, can you babysit him?' So I'm like, 'Fucking hell, all right, all right.' So I walk up the hall, and peer through the door and I see this kid sitting on the bed wearing like a plastic jacket, and I opened the door a bit and the room stank, and I mean *stank* of piss. I thought here we go, she must have meant *incontinent* not *intelligent*. I mean it was like rat's piss. So I went away, put a clothes peg over my nose, and went back and said hello. He was really polite and stuff and it turned out he had the window wide open and it was the river that stank of piss not him, it was actually coming up from the Thames."

PETE: "I'd have been 16 or 17 and my sister Amy-Jo returned from her first term at university and it was quite a big deal because the kind of upbringing I'd had, it was so strict that for her to be out there in the world doing as she pleased, well to this lonely foppish lad surrounded by barbed wire in a Warwickshire army camp, it was the stuff of fantasy. She gave me my first spliff and told me she'd met this fella called Carl who had long hair and a six-pack. I built up this picture in my mind before I met him: he was just Johnny Marr waiting for me to give him words.

"I was searching for this place, which people laughed at basically, that I'd always referred to as Arcadia and I just had this impression, I don't know *how*, I don't know *why*, that this fella wasn't gonna laugh. When I met him I think he did actually. Or was it I cried? I heard he was an amazing guitarist, so I had a vision of this partnership long before I actually encountered him, which would have been at Brunel in Richmond, right on the river."

CARL: "Straight away we were asking competitive, searching questions of each other. We had the dictionary out, seeing who knew the most words, and arguing for hours. Anyway, I hadn't picked up a guitar for six months, it was in the corner gathering dust, it was a disgrace. The other students would ask me to play Oasis, which was the nearest thing to my chording at the time. So Pete, what he did, and what he's *always* done, was he gave me a *reason* to do what I'd always *wanted* to do. Of course the first thing he wanted, in true Pete vein, was to show me what *he* could do.

"But in truth he could only play a couple of chords, so he played me this song he had called 'The Long Song', and as you can imagine it was fucking long! So what I did was I played it back to him but in barre chords which he'd never seen before so straight away he thought I was a fucking guitar legend.

"He was as drawn to the city as I was. I mean, London. He had nothing to offer but confidence, drive and persistence. The fact that he never shut up, pissed me off. He never stopped, he always carried on, but that persistence I admire in all people. He had a vision and he'd stop at nothing – he knew he was shit but he knew he'd get better."

PETE: "I tried to hang out with him but it was a case of being up all night with guitars on rooftops for one night, during which I'd set out all my inspiration and all my soul and it would ravage me, and then that would be it for, like, two or three weeks.

"I was born in Hexham but I never lived there. I lived in West London – Kilburn, Shepherd's Bush. Liverpool was where I always had a home. I'd lived in Krafeld, Nordrhine Westphalia in Germany. Ilford, Dorset, Coventry. I called Loftus Road home. The only life I knew was moving on, changing schools. Rootless? Absolutely. Particularly from 13 to 16 I was pretty much alone, living in dreams, kicking footballs against walls all day long. There was no nest to fly but wandering was in my nature. I was a fanatical journeyman – devoured literature, lived inside books and so on."

CARL: "I was born in Basingstoke to a London family. Everyone in my family had been born in London for generations except me and my sister who were unfortunately born in Basingstoke, which doesn't quite have the same ring to it. My parents were hippies who had jumped off the wagon in the Sixties, and they split up when I was about five. My dad moved to a council estate and tried to do writing jobs but to win bread they had to do factory jobs. My mum went the other way, she was a traveller and so I spent my life between this council estate and these hippy communes, so I was a veteran of the Battle of the Beanfield in '85 and was surrogate parented by Greenham Common ladies, stuff like that. Sort of a weird combination of pikey and new-age tosser.

"Pete went to uni to study English, and we both kind of used the whole further education thing as a means of getting money, a free ticket into London, into a new world. We made a pact together by a canal. I was very passionate, and totally disillusioned. One day I said to him, 'It's either the top of the world or the bottom of that canal,' and he said, 'Do you really mean what you're saying?' and that if I did, he would join me. I said, 'Yeah.'

"We decided to throw ourselves into eternity. I'd always felt like I'd lived a colourful, fraught, painful life and I had this in-built yearning for a feeling of security and some kind of friendship, above all that was the main thing. I was looking to calm down. I always saw myself as at the bottom, the scrubland, and I wanted to go somewhere that I could be proud. Make my Dad proud. Pete was from the opposite end. Fucking upsetting, manic unpredictability, and he was against anything and everything. So after I met him, I felt like I'd come to a crux."

PETE: "Something went badly wrong. I don't know what it was in me, some disease I think I was cured of not that long ago. People who you think you might fall in love with you try and hurt somehow. Not necessarily physically but emotionally, socially and brainiacally. All those early meetings were filled with spite and tension. It was fits and starts, boozy encounters in smoky little cellars, violent parties. He was just this wild fella, completely out of control which kind of drew me to him because there's no way in really.

"The odd occasion it was just me and him and a guitar he almost found it ridiculous that I was like open-mouthed at his ability. It was all alien to me. I didn't know anything about that world. Playing The Dublin Castle or The Bull & Gate was a fantasy. The idea of being onstage playing a guitar just never seemed possible. I was never a bedroom guitarist. I learned to play on the kerb, while trying to chat up birds, eating bad speed.

"With people like Carl who are very troubled and did their best to hurt me or make me uncomfortable, in many ways Carl's unique but in a lot of ways he's like a lot of people I met at that stage who put me down. But for him to call me shit was kind of the ideal, and for me to call him good . . . I don't know, he just lacked self-belief but I believed in him."

CARL: "We realised we were in it together. I'd done two years of drama, he'd done a year of English, we didn't want to end up at the bottom of that canal. I'd blagged every grant going just to stay alive. We'd beg, borrow and steal. We moved in together at the Holloway Road end of Camden Road. It was a guest house type of place, every kind of fucked-up weirdo you can imagine came by. At this stage, me and Pete were sharing a bed, a flea-bitten mattress, top to tail. It was a proper hovel."

PETE: "I was getting a band together one way or another, with or without him, but there was this nagging thing in the back of my mind that it *had* to be this fella. I suppose it wasn't for another year, after seeing him intermittently, when I moved to Whitechapel, that summer of 1998, that I tried to get hold of him. He was living in Stockwell looking after someone's house or something. I'd just taken my first job after leaving school as a gravedigger. Well, it was a machine that dug them and we filled them in, me and this old fella who taught me how to roll cigarettes. I needed saving, I was in a bad way. Carl came and saved me, he took me under his wings really, turned my life over. I left college which I hadn't really been at other than for my last year of grants. We ended up at Belinda's in Camden Road, top and tail on a single mattress. He still talks about the time he woke up with a fucking massive boner in his face. Obviously I knew nothing about it.

"Carl wanted us both to kill ourselves together at the same time. Get shotguns and shoot each other or jump off a high building. He'd had enough, he had this vision of himself that just kept reoccurring and it drove him, and me, insane. It was him, a dark bedsit, the windows closed, eating beans on toast and watching afternoon telly alone and broken. He reached a point where I couldn't get through to him. 'Death on the stairs,' that's what we called it."

CARL: "Scarborough Steve was our neighbour. He'd come round with his can of Special Brew. We weren't actively looking for a bass player, we were just looking for people like us, for libertines, though we didn't have the name then. We called ourselves The Strand and started recording demos. We'd go down to Food Records in Camden because we heard they had Blur, we'd bowl in there, charge up the stairs and play them our stuff. They laughed at us, we didn't care. All we wanted was some money. Funnily enough, EMI now publish our songs."

'SCARBOROUGH' STEVE: "I moved into a place called Delaney Mansions on Camden Road and they were already living there but we hadn't met each other. One night I'd gone out to a club on Tottenham Court Road, I was coming back on a 134 and I was on the top deck and so were they. I was with these two French birds and they thought I was some sort of French guy until they heard me say, 'Shut the fuck up,' or something, like in Yorkshire and they realised I was English and then they thought I was cool. So I staggered off the bus, and they staggered off the bus and we staggered to the same place and I was like, 'Ah, you live in my house? All right, cool, excellent,' but we didn't really say much, they went to their flat and I went to mine. Then I was sat in the garden reading this book on The Stooges and Pete came waltzing over with his guitar, so we started talking about music and hanging out from there in each other's flats.

"The first time I went into their flat Pete had been down to Dover and got a stack of beer that his mum had brought him, so we drank that and he said he wanted to get a band together. He was into The Beatles, Morrissey, Chas'n'Dave, The Velvet Underground and a lot of folky-sounding stuff, and like street-poet type stuff. It was always good but for me, I wanted to rehearse in a rehearsal room with a full band and electric guitars. Pete didn't care about that, he could just rehearse in his flat with his guitar. I didn't like doing it that way, I was used to playing with a band and it being pretty loud, you know? But Pete liked my songs and it was then that we said we should probably start a band."

ADAM EVANS (FOOD RECORDS A & R): "I was in The Good Mixer pub one night. Scarborough Steve comes up to me and says he's in this band and could I listen to his demo. He says, 'We're called The Libertines.'"

CARL: "Pete always has to know something you don't. So he'll say, 'I saw you once, like, on a bus – *but you didn't see me,*' just to have that secret one-up. There's a lot of animosity as to who came up with the name. Obviously I think it was me, but everyone else thinks it was them. Anyway we were in the basement one day and there was this book *The Lust of The Libertines* by the Marquis de Sade, so it was something to do with that."

PETE: "Why Carl would say that is absolutely beyond me. It's *my* book. I'd had it a while before I even met him. I'd read it when I used to come down to watch QPR on the train, and search for bohemia."

'SCARBOROUGH' STEVE: "I don't know who came up with it. Peter didn't know whether to call it The Albion or The Libertines, but I told him to call it The Libertines because that was way better, though The Albion would have been good as well."

ADAM EVANS: "I said, 'OK, come to the office the next day and play it to me.' So he came in, put it on the tape deck. He didn't seem pissed-up, he was just enthusiastic. So I listened to it but I couldn't really hear exactly what was going on. The recording was *terrible*, it was a really, really bad recording. He couldn't exactly sing and I couldn't tell what he was singing about, so I said, 'Nah, sorry Steve I can't sell this at the moment, I can't hear anything so take it back.' A few months later Carl and Pete came to the office to drop off a new demo, they were saying Steve's no longer in the band, so I thought, 'OK I'll give it a listen.' It was much better recorded than the one Steve had brought in. I remember thinking, 'Whoa, this is a bit different to what's going on at the moment.' 1997 we had bands like Blur, Dubstar and Grass Show doing well, but still hearing it and thinking, 'Yeah, it's a lot better but still not sure if Food Records could do anything with it.' Pete then came into the office on his own a few months later to say, 'Can I have my tape back. We've split up,' so I gave him his cassette back and that was that. 1997 wasn't their time. Now is their time."

PETE: "It was me, Carl and Steve. We believed in him. Steve was the leader of the band, he was our singer. We had the dream together. We had some right giffers on drums and bass. Justin, remember him? Fucking hell. It was the three of us then this fella called Justin came in and played bass. He was an Essex boy, a Mod. He promised us the earth. All he did was let us sleep in his girl-friend's bed, I had a dildo hanging out of my ear. Caused murders he did. Steve was trying to get us in with this bird who used to feed us acid and take us to parties in disused factories. We ended up living in one in the summer of love with Sandra the dancer. Justin appeared around then and caused a big rift. Steve had been living with the lad from Menswear, Johnny, and his bird Sheila out of Elastica. Anyway, Justin says he's written this song and starts singing it, going, 'I just wrote it, great innit?' Steve goes, 'Hang on, that's an Arthur Lee song,' and it was! It was 'Signed D.C.' off the first Love album. Justin didn't last long."

'SCARBOROUGH' STEVE: "He was playing bass and harpsichord, a bit of piano, on the first Libertines recording. We also used a drum machine on that. He'd tell stories and we just thought that some of them were slightly fucking tall. Like a fucking skyscraper.

"I met John Hassall *before* I met Pete and Carl. We hung out in The Good Mixer a few times, maybe went to a couple of clubs and gigs and stuff, or maybe just hung out round his mum's house a bit as well. So I told them he's got a wicked Rickenbacker and we can maybe rehearse in the basement at his mum's house. He was a good-looking guy and obviously talented in music. We needed a bass player and he was definitely the sort of guy I would go for. I took him over to Camden Road to their new place, introduced them and had a little jam and a few beers. Pete played 'Pay The Lady' and 'Dilly Boy'. We decided to carry it on, play together some more and start The Libertines."

CARL: "John Hassall was introduced to us by Scarborough Steve. He said, 'There's this kid, he's rich, good-looking, but above all he's got loads of equipment and a place to rehearse.' So we went to meet him in Camden at The Dublin Castle. He was sitting there with Johnny Borrell, wearing like a Beatles hat, a real train drivers' special. Initially I turned to Pete and said, 'Nah, he's too good-looking,' but needs must and all that.

"At first he was really wily, not too enthralled with what we were doing. He had his own agenda and was off to score some birds at The Monarch. I followed him along. Although he was really evasive he agreed to have us come around."

PETE: "John didn't talk that much because he was on about nine valium. He wasn't a wild child, he was stagnant really. I was amazed at the way his mum would give him money, I'd never seen anything like it. And the way he would talk to her, I'd have never have gotten away with talking to my mum like that. The fact he'd gone to a private school was a moot point with me and Carl. He had *amps* though. At first there was an enthusiasm there, a drive at that time but that disappeared. I think John just began to resent me, and maybe Carl too, I don't know. I was quite jealous of him and Carl actually."

CARL: "So we had a jam and he said he couldn't commit because he was in another band, but we weren't going to let that put us off because we'd found somewhere to rehearse. We showed him our songs which were like child's play to him because he was really accomplished even at that age. We spent the rest of the time playing Beatles songs. John kind of understood our vaguely skiffle-ish feel, which was quite surprising really, and he was always up for a melody, and always up for a knees-up. His mum used to put up with all manner of stuff. He used to have every bum around, every Kentish Town bum you can imagine, including yourself."

PETE: "We had this early song 'You're My Waterloo', he played bass along to it right away. You've got to remember I wasn't from a musical background. Jamming? I'd twitch if someone used that word. I never thought of myself as a musician, I wasn't that good. Anyone who could play in time and in tune to a song I'd written just blew me away."

CARL: "Pete was into Chas'n'Dave, Lindisfarne and The Smiths. I'd grown up with the Velvets, The Jam, and Buzzcocks. The Doors were also a big influence, The Beatles, Jackie Wilson. Pete read the *NME* and he knew what was going on. Me and Pete were the partnership, John was the master of the three-part harmony. We just used to rehearse in the basement and then go out on the lash together."

'SCARBOROUGH' STEVE: "Me and Carl would gatecrash parties. We stole a bottle of whisky from one, and managed to get a few lines of coke out of them before we got kicked out; we were *very* loud. Another party we went to uninvited we entered through a side window, rather than the front door."

ROGER SARGENT (BAND PHOTOGRAPHER): "The first time I came across them they lived above me in a flat on Holloway Road. Before they moved in we knew this prostitute living and working there, and she was fucking mental. We'd get knocks on the door from clients pretty much every day, ringing the wrong bell and stuff, and eventually, knowing that she and her prostitute cohort lived there, it was a bit weird when we started seeing hordes of young boys walking up and down the stairs. The guy I was living with was a music journalist and this prostitute hands him a demo of this band, The Libertines, and says she's the drummer. I think we threw it away [*laughs*].

"We used to go to this greasy spoon across the road and we'd see them sat there, really quietly, as I remember, in sort of black trench coats. It was Pete, Carl, Scarborough Steve, and quite possibly Johnny Borrell. It all got a bit sticky one night at about two in the morning. Someone was buzzing our door going, 'Can you let me in? Let me in.' So I say, 'Can I *fuck!* I don't even know who you are!' 'Oh, I live upstairs.' 'No you don't, so-and-so lives up there.' Next thing, he's kicked the front door down. So I run up, throw him down the stairs. I think it was Scarborough Steve but equally it could have been Pete or Carl. They moved out, and Peter claimed that the prostitute had attacked him with a pair of scissors, which is quite possible. I think Carl woke up one time and she was bobbing up and down on him. She was 29, but looked more like 49, rake-thin and very obviously a heroin addict. They were in good company right from the start!"

CHAPTER 2

Boys In The Band?

OCCASIONALLY Pete would pass by my mate's shop on Brick Lane and come in with an update or to leave some flyers for a forthcoming toilet gig. I certainly dug his sartorial sense, all ripped jeans, cycling tops and regulation mop-top, invariably with some exotic wastrel of a bird in tow. It was obvious a star was taking shape. Nevertheless, when he tried to pass a bent credit card to purchase a Mod-style parka I should have cuffed him there and then but already he had a loveable rogue air about him and he was simply told to fuck off, and that he'd have to get up a bit earlier if he was going to catch me out.

I remember another blot on his copybook was when he fervently began extolling the virtues of the two-tone band, The Specials, declaring them the best band ever. "Pah!" I thought. "Foolish youth!" I mean, everyone likes The Specials but when you start checking out the finer points of Can, Scott Walker, Funkadelic, Jonathan Richman, etc. the Coventry septet are decidedly school-yard stuff. Still, Pete had an engaging and infectious passion for rock 'n'roll that mirrors my own and I knew that he was one to watch.

Now based around a nucleus of Pete, Carl and John, with 'Scarborough' Steve something of a floating member, The Libertines extended their line-up, though not for the first or last time it would be anything but conventional.

CARL: "It was me, Pete, John and then we got Mr. Razzcocks on drums. At this stage I think he was 54, though it was rumoured he was older! [*laughs*] We weren't bothered about the image. We never wanted to be 'a band' we just wanted to play music. He was a character old 'Razzers', the only thing that got called into question was his addiction to baseball caps. Pete wanted him to wear a flat-cap. No one ever saw his head, but he was a very much involved member of the band. He was one of the boys.

"And then we added Vicky the Cellist, of noble blood. She was a young girl from the right side of the tracks who played cello. She was a natural, but she decided to rebel against being from the right side of the tracks and renounce her cello playing. She left of her own steam. The absence of cello didn't really hold us back though."

PETE: "She became a Mohican-wearing, squat-dwelling, bell-through-the-nose type. But Carl got what he wanted out of her. He ended up in this posh upper-middle class Notting Hill house. He just crashed there now and again, made her come, and her mum fed him up. I went round to see him one time with Francesca and absolutely disgusted him by fucking in the front room, and I got him evicted I think."

'SCARBOROUGH' STEVE: "I'd been kicked out of the flat because I was having to cash my own benefit cheques and sometimes the money wouldn't get to the right place, obviously. Pete and Carl let me stay at their new place, further up Camden Road. Our first gig was at that flat when the electricity ran out, so this German girl gave us 50p so we could get the gig back up and running, but later on Pete and Carl dressed up like Adolf Hitler and grabbed her in the toilets and really freaked her out. The second gig was at The Seen Bar, on Dean Street. We sat on barstools to play and I ended up falling off mine. I was always bladdered off my face, truly, truly bladdered."

PETE: "For the first time we weren't seeing Steve as the singer. Everything that happened at the brothel and The Empress of Russia led to Steve leaving. He disappeared completely off the map, leaving one of those plastic 75p footballs filled with speed, a big brass bed and a desk that I really wanted. I used to write, Steve hardly ever used to write so I needed that desk to certify something."

'SCARBOROUGH' STEVE: "We played a gig at The Empress of Russia in Angel, where I was living above in a squat. We weren't really very together. Everybody who lived in that squat went to Glastonbury and Carl, John, and Johnny Borrell also went, but I don't think I saw much of them there. I stayed longer than them at the festival. They came back and had recorded a demo. I get back, find out about it, call John and say, 'Have you guys recorded a demo?' He says, 'Yeah.' He sounded quite excited! [*laughs*] 'And you've got the singing on it?' 'Yeah.' 'So, what about me?' I asked. I was really pissed off about it. Maybe they just did the vocals because I wasn't there, but I took it as a hint that they didn't want me. I said, 'Right, I don't want to be in the band any more then,' and just put the phone down. I thought, 'Fuck that.' That was the first time I left the band."

PETE: "We spent that summer in Odessa Studios in Hackney with Gwyn, this Welsh fella who used to keep his eyes open with matchsticks, a proper old school engineer. He'd done the first Pistols demo, let them in the back door. We didn't have a drummer though. So this Welsh fella says, 'I know this old geezer who'll play the drums for you for 50 quid,' and half an hour later Mr. Razzcocks walked in the door. We did our first demo, a song called 'Pay The Lady'.

"'Pay The Lady', 'Breck Road Lover' named after the area of Liverpool my family comes from by Anfield, and 'Music When The Lights Go Out'. Our first proper gig was at The Hope & Anchor on

19

Upper Street on September 11, 1999. We did seven or eight songs. Mr. Razzcocks wouldn't stand for any second-rate playing. It was a kind of a benchmark for me in terms of my family. To them I'd just been bumming around and all my talk of psychedelia and arcadia didn't wash, but doing gigs meant suddenly we are a *band*.

"We were like The Bootleg Beatles with a 70-year-old drummer and a fucking weird cellist. 'Razzers' was looking for wedding gigs. We'd play God knows where, old people's homes. We were going to play 'Hey you, get off of my cloud' to the old folks. John was into that."

CARL: "We got our first mention in the *NME* around this time. It said we were 'fresh, wry, flowery and savage'. Roger Morton had showed an interest in managing us, and we liked the kudos of his *NME* status. We thought we were in then, that it would be all plain sailing from there. How wrong we were! We'd play anywhere. We had to blag to get the gigs, and then we'd end up having to pay for them.

"I don't know what happened with Morton, it just sort of fizzled out. He was with us about a year, though it was a very hands-off style of management. I think he got us one gig, at Blow-Up, and took us to meet some poncey record company executives who definitely did *not* like us, which was fair enough I suppose. Morton just kind of lost interest. I think I had about one conversation a month with him on average."

PETE: "We weren't bothered about 'Razzers' being 55 or what-ever, we didn't have a cynical game plan, that came in later in full effect with Banny. We were lost in songs. At that stage we didn't really look outside our little rabbit hole. I was working in a bar, selling drugs, working on a building site. Writing poetry in the graveyard shift at The Kings Head and spanking off old queens for, like, 20 quid. I did it a couple of times, yeah. I remember once being taken back to this mews house in Chelsea, right old fucking badger he was. Fucking hell. It was a bit daft actually; I used to fancy myself as the character from *Suedehead*. As he slept I locked him in his room, tied a pair of trousers over his head and nicked all these American dollar bills out of his drawer. He's probably still there, with a hard-on, listening to Classic FM.

"I was putting on a lot of what I called 'Arcadian Cabaret Nights', down at The Foundry on Old Street, and the old Finnegans Wake – you must mention that place. It was my main outlet as a poet, as a writer. I was getting a lot from London. Stranded in the infinite dawn. I don't know if you know about the wards; a ward is the ancient term for the boroughs of London, and, in particular, the City of London. Even just three or four streets would contain its own dialect, its own culture, even its own flag. So we'd wander the wards.

"Although the fascination with London did extend to, and this might sound far-fetched, but as part of the Arcadian Cabaret, I found myself in Russia for a short time, and I definitely left something behind in Moscow. That's not some corny play on lyrics, there was a good part of me found an awakening in Moscow, a liberty I've never known anywhere. It was pure Arcadian reverie. I was faced with a choice: if you wanna dive in the river, dive in the river son, you'll freeze to death but go on, it might be a giggle. Making love in these huge Stalin tenements with the bed falling through the floor. Cold, cold, cold. The fascination for London did extend to Liverpool as well, spending summers up there with my nan, and St. Petersburg for some reason, although I've never made it there yet. Somehow I know I'll end up in St. Petersburg, in a high-ceilinged room with elongated windows."

CARL: "There was a glimmer of hope when we started doing our Filthy's thing. We started to get a reputation as faces, in a local way, playing all the time at Filthy McNasty's, where Pete was an occasional barman. Then [music lawyer] Banny Poostchi turned up, [sometime in late spring 2000] which was the start of a new epoch. What got us interested was she worked for Warner Chappell Music Publishing, and had been a lawyer for Oasis, and what got her interested was the spirit of it really; she was won over by our spirit. Of course she started rowing with Pete right away. I mean she got us a photo-shoot with a near blind guy – but the photos were really good! That gives you an idea of the hotchpotch absurdity of it all. Then eventually John got fed up with Pete's willy-nillyness, and doing random silly little gigs, so he left the band. There was always a lot of friction about gigs. John wanted to play a gig at The Monarch and Pete had booked another at Filthy's and that's what split the band. Madness really, but that's what led to the [first] going of separate ways."

PETE: "Yeah, Banny came along, she was impressed by what we were doing. This fur coat walked into the pub, with hockey sticks for legs. Like an ambassador's wife crossed with a scarecrow – very beautiful, very intelligent, though her main attraction was Steve. She wasn't from our world, from our culture, but she saw Steve and loved his hairstyle. But this was when we were starting to pull away. Basically Carl didn't want to be in a band with Steve, he thought he was vulgar. Banny paid for us to do a demo, a song called 'Love On The Dole' which to this day I think is one of our greatest songs."

CARL: "I was a bit irked as I thought it would have been more profitable to have done the gig at The Monarch. John was into furthering careers and all that and just said he couldn't do it any more and 'Razzers' went with him. I was narked with Pete at the time, for fucking it up."

PETE: "It was also to do with the brown as well. At that stage I'd started taking it a lot. Basically I had this amazing china white heroin which you don't get in London. This fella I knew had smuggled it back from India up his arse. I told John about it. It was stupid of me to tell him about it as he'd had a hard time giving it up a couple of years earlier but he said, 'OK, let's get high.' I'd never seen him like that. He was all ready to go back into it. But I was disgusted with myself so I threw it down a drain as a gesture. From that moment on it was just a matter of time. I was selling a lot of speed, a lot of weed."

CARL: "We were still living in this skanky little basement, absolutely hated by the people who lived above. Even the woodshed had been rented out, a little coal bunker under the steps to a French conceptual artist who lived in it. Our only ambition was to not be in the same position in 30 years' time. Our mission was to just get paid for doing music. We held some of the best parties Camden has ever known."

PETE: "Carl started living at Johnny Borrell's mum's and I lived in a Peabody cottage in Tottenham with Steve. We had no full-time drummer, no bass player, and at that time I felt isolated by Carl's reluctance to rehearse, to meet up even. He was involved in quite a tempestuous relationship at the time and I wasn't particularly welcome at his place, and that was when the rot set in really; that was the beginning of the end for me and Carl – that year before we got signed when we didn't see each other at all. I don't think we grew apart, neither of us did *any* growing. He became a bit disillusioned with me and the path I was taking. He wasn't staying in tune to what we'd always believed in. We couldn't get on at all, couldn't be in each other's company without bickering."

'SCARBOROUGH' STEVE: "I was living with Pete in Tottenham. We had mad times. I remember once he had this big automatic sort of estate car. We were skint one night so we drove down the West End and pretended to be a taxi cab firm and took some people back to their houses and got money for it. We made about 30 quid, went to McDonald's for burgers and went home. About a year after I'd left the band I wasn't doing very much. I'd been mulling about, getting too drunk, taking too many drugs, but I'd been hanging out with them still and we started playing together again.

"Second time around we were rehearsing almost every day, in Whitechapel at Pete's pad, usually smoking pure opium spliffs. It really was just me and him. I didn't see Carl or John the whole time, that second time. We were doing 'Time For Heroes' and 'Mayday', I even believe that one of the tapes that got to the record company had me singing on it, on a few of the songs that were on the first album.

"I got frustrated because every day it was me and Pete playing, I don't think Carl turned up very much. They were catty all the time with each other, a lot of the time it was little arguments and getting at each other."

CARL: "Banny came back to me and Peter and said, 'Get it back together, we can fucking *do* this.' [Around September 2001] we blagged Gary on the drums through Banny."

Banny Poostchi started managing the original line-up (i.e. with Razzcocks on drums) after Morton left in late spring 2000, having met the band through Alex Clarke at Filthy McNasty's. She was excited by their talent– but not so excited by the road they were going down – light, skiffle based acoustic songs and she left in winter 2000. Later on the band split up – John and Razzcocks went their separate ways, but Carl and Peter still nursed the dream. In late summer 2001, they hooked up again with Banny, who this time was confident of getting them signed – but they would have to write a new body of songs – songs like 'Horror Show', 'Up The Bracket' and 'Time For Heroes', that took the delicate balladry of before but would now twist it through a heavier, more energetic, snarling rock. She brought Gary in on drums (around September 2001) to help shape the new sound which all four developed throughout a feverish rehearsal period until late November 2001. Only when they were properly ready was Banny prepared to let any labels see them.

PETE: "Gary had started rehearsing with us but he refused to commit himself. He was non-committal, but high on energy in the rehearsals. He held the band together in a way, made me very aware of what I was doing and it was something new to me. I'd never worked like that before, I was learning so much. I wanted to prove to him that I could play. To Banny's horror, me and Carl had decided that Steve wasn't going to be in the band any more, full stop. She adored him, she spoiled him – wore him on her arm like a little prize."

'SCARBOROUGH' STEVE: "The one rehearsal I did as a full band with Gary I was absolutely pissed so it didn't go very well. I was digging my own grave really. I'd started modelling with *Select* and left the band to go to New York to work. I was probably never going to be involved in it. I was just helping Pete do his songs as I was his friend at the time. I never understood quite why he wanted me anyway because they were his songs and he sang them in his way; it was pointless me doing it 'cos he could do it better. When I joined in the first place the thing that got to me was Pete wanted me to sing the songs exactly how he did, in his voice almost and I didn't want to do that. But I wanted to join the band so I went along with it. I wanted to make up the melodies, because otherwise I'd have no input, so that was a problem from the very start. I was always doomed to failure 'cos I wasn't into that."

'Scarborough' Steve left The Libertines for the last time, though the real reason for his permanent exile is, typically, cloaked in confusion.

Steve clearly feels he was pushed, though Pete would later tell *Guitar* magazine that Steve jumped on account of the band not being "New York Dolls enough."

Another of John Hassall's friends was Johnny Borrell, a game young buck who'd go on to form Razorlight under the tutelage of one-time Libertines manager, Roger Morton. I first encountered genial Johnny at John's mum's, and watched with amusement his various mutations over the next few years as he strove to carve out a niche for himself. So you're listening to Gram Parsons, Johnny? Cowboy hat: check. Bob Dylan? Walk down Kentish Town Road with a weighty volume of obscure poetry under your arm: check. Tom Verlaine now? Wholesale sonic thievery: fucking check! I remember giving the young whippersnapper some advice on building up his upper body strength by doing press-ups correctly. He was getting sand kicked in his face, and by the next time I saw him, on Hampstead Heath with his top off, he'd filled out a bit and could have done a paper bag a bit of damage, wet or otherwise. By the time Razorlight arrived, he'd teamed up with some despicably pretentious Swedish kids who lorded it up like they were in fucking U2 because they'd got a record deal. He quickly got himself a rep as a bit of a big-head motormouth after likening himself to Dylan in an early interview, though I was impressed that he didn't play up his Libertines connection when many others, including Dominic from The Others, can't do any press without namedropping Pete.

For all his crimes against humility, I was as impressed as everyone else when his debut offering 'Up All Night', which reeked of the CBGB's bands I adored, crashed into the Top Five. If it was a three-way fuck between Tom Verlaine, Patti Smith and Richard Hell, at least the sex was good. That said, on one track, I winced as he sang the line "the streets that I grew up on, they may mean nothing to you" like a New York street-gutter poet talking about the Lower East Side, when he could only have been referring to Hampstead Garden Suburb.

Three years earlier, the boy Borrell's career was following a far different trajectory . . .

CARL: "Johnny Borrell, well *he actually approached me* and said he'd play bass, so I said, 'I know for a fact you've got your own shit bubbling,' but he said, 'No, no I can do it.' In fact I remember rehearsing him up on the bass on September 11 to put a timescale on it. So we rehearsed up four songs prior to our meeting James [Endeacott, Rough Trade] to get signed. Then I phoned up Borrell to say I was on my way to the studio to do the showcase thing and said, 'Where are you?' He said, 'Oh, I'm in Cardiff on a tour bus with Alabama 3, having the high life.' 'So are you coming?' 'No.'"

PETE: "I'd put together a demo. Carl didn't show much interest. He came over to my gaff in Whitechapel. We did 'Mockingbird' and two songs which didn't really fit in with Banny's idea of what we should present to Rough Trade. She just said, 'I *will* get you signed to Rough Trade.' But then along came James from a little indie label called High Society, and said, 'Wicked songs, love it, I wanna release it.' It was the first time someone had come along and wanted to release our music. He said he'd give us a grand. I was amazed but could see he was genuine. He used to come down to our rehearsals, and bring booze. It was me, Carl, Gary, James and Banny. I don't think they hit it off as individuals and she had no interest in what she called a 'tin-pot label', she worked for Warner and dealt in the big league. I was like, 'Fuck it let's just get it out there.' We then did some demos of 'Horrorshow', 'Time For Heroes', 'Never Never', 'General Smuts', 'East Of Eden' on James' girlfriend's sister's 4-track in North London, a girl called Vicky Churchill. Banny took those demos and made sure they got to Rough Trade."

27

JAMES MULLORD (HIGH SOCIETY RECORDS): "Somebody dropped me a tape, it had three tracks on it 'Mockingbird', 'Looking Glass' and another I can never remember. I met Pete, Carl and Johnny [Borrell] who was in the band at the time, and was charmed by them instantly. Pete didn't turn up to our first meeting because he'd been busted in Liverpool and was in the cells after a big night out. I had a very, very abrasive early relationship with Banny. Pete was saying, 'Oh, we're going to sign to High Society,' and Banny just walked up to me in the pub one day and really aggressively went, 'They aren't signing to *you*,' right in my face and I just went, 'Hey, I'll make an offer. If you don't want it, that's fine, all right?'

"I didn't have a lot of experience, didn't really know what to do with it. You could tell you had two really talented characters there but we didn't have the wherewithal or knowledge to know what to do with it. Banny really kicked their arse, bought them a guitar, a bass, and gets them a drummer and pulled it all together. It was Banny, no doubt about it, who nailed them that deal."

CARL: "Borrell fucking let us down like a trooper! Luckily, and in the face of adversity, we pulled it off anyway with me and Pete swapping the bass and Gary on drums. I was disappointed with Johnny though, I said to him, 'I can see this isn't your bag, are you gonna do it or are you gonna let us down?' He said he would and then he put us in the shit. He had his own fish to fry and I said to him, because of that, I didn't see him in our band but he insisted he could handle it. Mind you, the idea of him *and* Pete, I mean no fucking stage is big enough for those two egos!"

JAMES MULLORD: "Johnny always wanted to be a frontman. I thought he was a really good little guitar player but he'd get drunk and be really rude – really nice until he got pissed, then he'd just get really arrogant. He still owes me a tenner, by the way."

PETE: "I approached Borrell and asked him to play, told him I was putting down the guitar. He was a friend but I don't think he had a great deal of respect for our friendship. He was arrogant, and that's not me bitching. But me and Johnny spent a lot of time together at that stage. He'd just moved into Brick Lane and I was living in Whitechapel and I remember long days in his flat with him.

"I learned a lot from him actually, he seemed to have sorted himself out. He had quite a good little band coming on, he was really developing as a guitar player and I respected that, a lot of finger-picking and shit. I said, 'Do you wanna help us out for a bit playing bass?' and he did one rehearsal then fucked off somewhere when we were supposed to be doing a gig.

"What kept us going was strong ideas and passion. It was fucking skagged-up, desperate passion. We were angry by this stage as well. Sick of it. Skint. Carl was really down on his luck, kipping on sofas, split up from his missus. Fucked off. Lads were coming over in American bands and sweeping up. We were terrible. This was November 2001. Still me, Carl and Banny are plotting away. She said she'd get us signed to Rough Trade and suddenly they put us in the studio to demo some songs."

JAMES ENDEACOTT (ROUGH TRADE RECORDS): "This girl kept calling me about this band The Libertines who I'd never heard of, saying, 'You've got to come and see them. They're amazing.' So she arranged to meet me at 6 o'clock at the office, and she turned up in a flash car, not a limo but a real sort of fancy car. I'd never met the girl before, but I got in the car and she was really full-on, she had loads of bags of crisps and nuts and, like, beer and loads of cans of Coca-Cola in case I didn't drink! I was going to go and meet the band in a rehearsal space just off Old Street, and as we were driving there she kept telling me how these two guys were going to be the new Lennon and McCartney, and the new Jagger/Richards, and how this guy Pete was like Elvis, and just basically bigging them up with the biggest names ever in rock, so I just knew I was going to be completely deflated because it was obvious nothing could live up to that.

"So I walk in there and see these three guys; Gary's like this muscleman behind the kit and he starts talking in this weird New Jersey-stroke-Birmingham accent and then there's Pete and Carl who were both quite charming. So they say, 'Do you want to hear something?' and they played me four songs – 'Time For Heroes', 'Up The Bracket', 'Boys In The Band' and maybe 'I Get Along', or it might have been 'Horrorshow' actually. Well, the energy I got from it, and also the words which I got a lot of and thought were amazing, and the catchiness of the tunes, and also just the presence of Pete and Carl, it was *amazing*. They said, 'Is there anything you wanna ask us?' and I said, 'Yeah, can I hear those four songs again?' So they play them again and I was pretty blown away, didn't know *what* to think. So as I was leaving Banny gave me this CD with one song on it, 'Mockingbird', so I said goodbye and said I'd be in touch and I'm walking down to Old Street station thinking, 'Fucking hell, I've got this CD, I've *got* to listen to it,' and put it on my Walkman and it's just these weird loops and samples and bits of talking on it, *completely* the opposite of what they'd just played for me, so it really sort of threw me.

"About a month later I get a call from Banny saying they're doing a gig tonight at The Rhythm Factory in Whitechapel, but I'm already going to see one of our artists, Cara Dillon, this Irish folk singer at The Spitz club. We all went from work, and I got a bit drunk, but as it was just round the corner I decided to go to The Rhythm Factory. I asked a few people to come down with me but they were all like, 'No, it's gone midnight,' or whatever, and I saw Geoff and Jeanette driving off. Anyway, I walked into The Rhythm Factory and it was like walking into *this whole new world*. I mean, there are all these people I've never met before, and it's obvious there's something going on; it was full of weird and wonderful people, sort of freaks, and total bohemians. The band came on at about two in the morning, it was incredibly hot and sweaty, they had just the one microphone and they played about six songs, just the three of them, and I *remembered* the words and *knew* the songs as soon as they came in – I was just so, so excited. I was getting feelings that I thought had gone, feelings like when I first saw bands that I'd forgotten about. It was like seeing The Beatles in Hamburg in 1962, it was mind-blowing. I couldn't believe how good it was.

"I went into work on Monday and just kept going on at Geoff about them. He said, 'Let's give them some money and make a little demo.' They went into Nomis [Studios] and did four songs and it was just unbelievable; the lyrics, the energy, it was like The Kinks meets The Beatles. It was really English but also kind of like The Strokes. I said to Geoff, 'We've got to do it, we've got to do it.'"

GEOFF TRAVIS (ROUGH TRADE RECORDS): "I was just glad to see James so excited about a band. He's got really good musical taste, it's not usual for him to be raving about bands. He said he thought they were a classic band with great songs; we all love The Kinks and The Who and that sort of line of English bands, and James said they were in that vein. We went to see them rehearse and it was love at first sight. I didn't need convincing at all – it's nice when that happens."

PETE: "We had a showcase for Geoff [Travis], Jeanette [Lee] and James [Endeacott] at a rehearsal room in Bermondsey. It was difficult to gauge their reactions but Jeanette said, 'We're going to sign you,' and she seemed to speak for all of them. We rolled up the street with our guitars over our shoulders, and we went to The Players Bar, under the theatre in Charing Cross Road and just got rotten. For the first time me and Carl opened up to Gary and said, 'It's gonna happen, mate.' It was ecstasy. It was what we wanted. It was the happiest moment of my life easily. We were really buzzing, really confident, but that night Gary wouldn't commit. He was still playing with this other band and said he couldn't say for definite."

CARL: "I'd still see John. I went to see his Bob Dylan-style gigs with the gospel singers. It was unavoidable; that whole Camden scene, we all shot from the same gun really. Hassall actually got back in touch with *us*, after he heard we'd got signed. It was a bit weasel-like, the way he did it. We were a man short, we needed four men, so I don't blame him for getting back in touch. I mean, anyone would really."

PETE: "I was in the kitchen in Dalston, I don't think he realised how upsetting that phone call was. John called and said, 'If you need a bass player I'd be interested.' I broke down. He left us when we really needed him. I was crying but we decided we'd bite the bullet and get him back in on bass. My first choice didn't want to play, a boy called Jai Stanley. He'd started playing semi-professional foot-ball and didn't want to move to London."

CARL: "So we said to John if he wanted this job, it was his, but it was a *job*, and this time there'd be none of our old happy-go-lucky boys, this time it's blood, and when I say you play downstrokes you play fucking downstrokes until your fingers bleed, 'cos that's what we're about now. Downstrokes are harder to do and you feel pain doing it. We said, 'Look, you let us down but welcome back, but *this* is your job if you wanna be a part of it.'

"We started calling him 'Mr. Lombard' 'cos it was just the most drab, English-sounding name. Pete was Mr. Spaniel. We had differ-ent guises, silly accents, just attention-seeking stuff really. Pete started talking like a rude-boy and calling himself 'Leroy the Fox', John was 'Delroy the Antelope', and I was 'Wise Owl'. John, or 'Delroy', had taken up the viola and one day we were getting the tube from Kentish Town, the three of us, and he had this long trench coat, a face like death and these little blue, round sunglasses. And, of course, this viola case.

"Obviously we didn't have any funds so we didn't have any tickets, and John managed to get collared by a guard, but he decided to make a break for his liberty. Me and Pete were clean away, but John was legging it down the escalator with a fluorescent-jacketed guard in hot pursuit. This was clearly the most excitement the guy had had all week, so he was hell-bent on snaring Delroy the Antelope. Anyway, he still had his viola case which looked like a machine gun, I mean he looked like some sort of assassin. He gets down one side then he legs it up the other, with a beam like a Cheshire cat laughing at this guard, but the guy runs up after him. So he gets to the top of the escalator and then he slides down the middle bit, and gets clobbered in the nuts by the 'stop' signs, flies off and breaks his ankle! He ended up limping to our destination, so that became known as the legend of Delroy's lame hoof.

"There was a lot of umm-ing and aah-ing, lots of 'will-they, won't-they?' We thought we'd blagged it but we were that scared that we got off at the wrong tube station on our way to sign the deal. We'd jumped the tube but we'd got off at the wrong stop, we were shitting ourselves, running round the bleak streets and blandness of West London trying to find the fucking office. We couldn't find the Westway and we're saying, 'That's it, they're gonna change their minds without a doubt.' When we got there, there was a cake, a bottle of champagne and a fat line of yellow bugle waiting for us. Anyway, from that day forth, things went downhill. I think that was the start of the demise of The Libertines."

JAMES ENDEACOTT: "Me, Geoff and Jeanette were thinking, 'Are they gonna turn up?' because it was the last day of work before Christmas and everyone had gone home early, and they were about an hour late. Little did I realise that was the way it was going to be with them! It was a really memorable time. I used to go out with them a lot, to places like Filthy's and met this whole new world. Martin, from Selfish Cunt, and Dominic from The Others, it was full of people who wanted to be something, but it felt like they were all quite happy just saying to each other, 'You're great.' What Pete and Carl did, though unbeknown to them at the time, by signing the deal they slowly stepped out of that scene. I'd find myself at home on a Saturday and I'd say to my wife Jill, 'I've just got to go to Filthy's.' I'd fallen under their spell.

"Another great time, I was on the tube with Pete and Carl, they were both wearing trilbys, going into the East End on the Hammersmith & City line, when there was some sort of problem and we got stuck in the tunnel. They just started to sing and dance for the whole carriage, and they had the place in hysterics. I thought, 'I've met the Artful Dodgers here', they were just so Dickensian, so cheeky and charming, clever, smart and witty. I was just *completely* under their spell. They took it really calmly, but now I realise they were quite blown away at the thought they were getting signed."

GEOFF TRAVIS: "It was the usual waiting [*laughs*]. But we thought it was worth waiting for and they did eventually show up. It's difficult to get Peter to sit down, to sit still and talk to you – there's lots of jumping around and clowning around. They were hugging Banny and lifting her off the floor. It was a great moment for them, they felt recognised and we were just glad to be the ones to do that."

Pete Doherty would later describe signing the Rough Trade deal as both the best and the worst day of his life . . .

PETE: "Best in terms of the opportunity to realise our potential. You've got to understand that just being in a position to record a song – well, that was pure fantasy. Even having our own guitars seemed almost impossible. It was a dream. Carl did promise me years earlier that the day we got signed he'd roll me a massive booner, which was what we called a spliff with heroin in it, weed, everything in it all at once. I think he's still making it."

CARL: "Because of the implications that it led to, and the fucking erroneous confidence it affords you, and just the slacking that it allows you, you know, it takes all the wind out of your sails, and that goes hand-in-hand with fucking drugs. We had access, we had the key. That Christmas the money came in, for the first time in our lives we had credit in the bank, and that was the key to a world of better drugs, and a constant supply of them."

CHAPTER 3

The Albion Sails . . .
On Course?

THE Libertines had sprung up seemingly overnight, though of course they'd been honing their craft for a good few years. Theirs was a name that had been fairly well known on the London gigging circuit but laughed at in a way. Now, with the word on the street that they'd been signed, people suddenly talked about the band in more hallowed terms. By the spring of 2002, the *NME* began furiously courting The Libertines in a relationship that has grown exponentially, although they surely could never have envisaged just how many future column inches they'd garner.

As early as May 2002 'What A Waster' would entrench itself in the higher reaches of the paper's "Turn Ons" section for weeks on end, with the band being billed as "East London's sharply dressed sons" and "brash, bold and brilliant cockney upstarts", signalling the start of an inextricable link between The Libertines and the capital which I found quite amusing given that only John Hassall could be described as a real Londoner.

Since inking the Rough Trade deal in the Christmas of 2001, Pete would stop by my mate's shop with money to spend and tales of support slots with band-of-the-moment The Strokes and I thought, "Good for you, chaps." I was especially pleased for John. I'd still to see or hear anything of their newly recorded output, so it was with some trepidation that I bought the debut 'What A Waster' single from Virgin in Notting Hill Gate. I really hoped it would live up to my expectations. I wasn't disappointed.

'What A Waster' was an instant classic; pure punk rock swagger with a lyrical deftness that pointed to great things. I mused over who it could be about and couldn't help but put 'Scarborough' Steve in the frame, though in time it would become eerily autobiographical, coming largely from the pen of Pete Doherty.

Daytime radio banned it immediately for its surfeit of "fucks", "piss" and the dreaded c-word, though an edited version became 'Single of the Week' on Mark Radcliffe's Radio 1 show. The furore ensured that it scraped into the Top 40 by the skin of its foul-mouthed teeth, despite very little having been heard or written about the band up to this point. Already, Pete was giving the press a taste of what was to come, making oblique but topical references to the Taliban, and a tale about a previous bass player who had run off to join them, which may or may not have been true.

If 'What A Waster' swaggered, the flipside offering 'I Get Along' burst out of the traps with genuine breakneck rama-lama-lama punk rock balls. It was sexy, full of angst and could have been written and recorded by any of the band's great punk and new wave forebears. Similarly, the fresh, direct and urgent 'Mayday', clocking in at about one minute, at first seemed an afterthought but served to showcase Pete and Carl's call-and-response vocal interplay which would become a recurring feature of their work, and is one of the ingredients I personally enjoy. Live it was an incendiary, blink-and-you'll-miss-it experience.

PETE: " 'Mayday' is *The Likely Lads'* theme tune crossed with the *Steptoe And Son* theme tune."

I must have listened to those three songs five or six times on the bounce with the volume cranked to the max. I loved it. At a stroke (no pun intended), they rendered all the new (and not-so-new) bands dickless and impotent. The single was bereft of any phoniness. It was clearly the real deal.

In Doherty and Barat, there seemed to be the crucial components found in any great partnership: respect, competition and the joyous spunkiness of youth. Only later would the world at large discover just how complex their relationship was.

PETE: "First of all we say, 'We want to get new guitars, and we want a 24-hour rehearsal room, can you do that for us?' And I remember actually, in my mind, being distinctly quite assertive in a way that surprised even myself. I was very adamant that this should be done properly and that our demands be met, and that's why we signed to Rough Trade primarily. It wasn't the most money but we were under the impression we were going to have artistic freedom and they'd appreciate us as artists.

"We started rehearsing at Ruse in Old Street. The plan was being formulated by Banny and Rough Trade. After Christmas, me and Carl went straight in and said we wanted a place to live together. That time leading up to the deal and straight after the deal was the first time we could be in the same room together."

TONY LINKIN (COALITION PR): "James Endeacott invited me round to Rough Trade to listen to some tracks and after that I went down to the studio and thought they were amazing. I met them all as well and thought they were great characters. Pete and Carl seemed very cheeky. Peter, I remember, kissing me the first day and being very charming. We just hit it off immediately. I thought they sounded great – and they *were* great."

PETE: "The plan was to get a load of money but it was frustrating when, in reality, it didn't materialise. It did come, in fits and starts. There were contractual stipulations, and me, Carl and Banny decided it would be 10 grand spent on equipment and the guitars of our dreams. You know, just having ten B&H in your pocket and enough for a pint or to go and see a film was like a big deal."

TONY LINKIN: "The dynamic was amazing. It's always what's been really special about them. Carl is probably the one that you can get on with easier, but I love them both for what they are, they're both very funny. They would antagonise each other quite a bit, shall we say. The pair of them together have got such a sense of humour; they're like brothers, like Liam and Noel [Gallagher], in that way they can argue a hell of a lot and then make up."

ROGER SARGENT: "I was about to quit the whole business, I'd had enough. I'd had enough of bands, of music, and just working in the business completely. I'd already moved out of London, I'd taken a new job out of London, and a couple of my friends were trying to convince me to stay, and Tony [Linkin] was one of them. He and James Oldham said, 'Come and see this band.' So I went down to Cherry Jam thinking, 'Oh, you know it's just another job,' and was just blown away. At the end of the gig, I said to Tony, 'I *have* to do this band.' I kept on at him for about a month afterwards and then did the first press shots.

"In the preceding five or six years there was nothing that challenged me, they were the first band I'd seen for years that excited me *and* scared me at the same time. For me that's the whole essence: I don't *want* to know what's going to happen next, and they had that unpredictability. They had a bit of a scuffle onstage which obviously wasn't planned, and they had really good songs. Plus, when I walked into the club I looked around and said to myself, 'Right, *he's* got to be in the band . . . *he's* got to be in the band, etc, etc,' and I picked them all without even meeting them. They looked *fantastic*, and then all the pictures I got, they looked like The Beatles in Hamburg."

PETE: "That was the first gig playing as the four-piece which everyone has come to know and love as The Libertines, everyone except me of course. It was the first convergence on a venue of what became our *gang*, really. There was something in the air that night, I don't know if there was a full moon, but that venue/that night played host to all our mates, minders, mugs and minions that came to frequent The Albion Rooms over the next six months, and just general debauchery ensued. I remember getting thrown out with Left Hand after the gig and that set the standard.

"Our first proper manager, Banny, she oversaw it all really; introduced us to different press teams, and different photographers. The infrastructure that stands today as being at The Libertines' roots since entering the industry is the one that Banny brought together – it's her legacy. Some very strange people, indeed.

"Playing with The Strokes was almost the ideal – I suppose it was in a way. I first bumped into them through this lass I'd been Bonnie and Clyde-ing with for a few years called Francesca, and just as things were falling apart with her, things were coming together with the band. I don't think that's coincidence, to be honest, but she introduced me to The Strokes when I was still on the dole in Whitechapel. I got some tickets and went up with Mairead and Carl to Liverpool.

"Me and Carl got done actually by one of their security guards – got a bit of a clip round the ear for trying to nick their guitar pedals. We ended up supporting them at Leeds and Birmingham; there were about three heads bopping up and down during 'Time For Heroes'. My abiding memory of that is hearing this New York voice going, 'Peter, are you trying to give me *crack*?' – it was Julian – at this point, I still hadn't smoked crack, that was to come later. But I did have a rock, having scored on the street in King's Cross some coke, ended up with this rock of crack but I didn't know what to do with it, I just had it in my little tin.

"The Strokes were just exploding, getting massive and they were a bit wary, they certainly weren't lording it. Unfortunately the people that were around us, who'd come up on tour with us really, *they* were lording it. This posh fella came in the dressing room and said [*adopts upper-class accent*], 'I say, have you got a big dick?' to one of The Strokes, and they were a bit like, 'Er, who the fuck's this prick?' and so it was a bit of a shame."

CARL: "It was The Strokes, I suppose, who pissed us off in the first place really by coming to our country, wearing our clothes, having our audience with our women and our excitement! They're a funny bunch, very cautious. We blagged two gigs with them through James Endeacott which at the time was delightful news because to be fair we did very much admire and enjoy their record, and it was also a wake-up call to us."

PETE: "I remember Brighton with The Vines, fucking hell, 'Scarborough' Steve decided he was back in the band – ended up losing another tooth. Carl hit him with his guitar, and afterwards, he ran up to Carl on the beach while we were having a midnight session and Carl got a kick in the knackers from Steve and they had a massive scrap, and then Steve disappeared. Got on a train and went back to Scarborough for about six months.

"We were starting to play to fair-sized audiences all the time and me and Carl entered into this strange world of paranoia, feelings of paranoia and over-analysis; being aware that people know who you are, and who you *think you are*. And something as simple as Craig Nicholls from The Vines coming down and listening to our soundcheck, and *dancing* to our soundcheck, really set me at ease, and ever since then, it's always been really important that support bands, and bands we go on tour with, are good people. They *do* wanna have a jam, they *do* wanna listen to the music, get to know each other. Yeah, that quite impressed me and whatever happened since then, whatever tantrums he had and when he didn't give me much weed, I'll always remember him in his little Adidas top dancing around to 'Boys In The Band'. I didn't see anything of his supposed madness, what I did see signs of was the people around him giving him every opportunity to act like that, excluding people from him that maybe he might have liked to have met. No one's ever been able to control *me* like that."

CARL: "With The Vines it was kind of disheartening for me, they were equally cautious. I'd always wanted the bands we played with to be like being in The Yardbirds, in the Sixties – a sense of sharing and a sense of community. I was of the opinion that we were all blaggers and we'd all managed to end up in this place where we could make some sort of difference. But everyone was very cautious, and would want to defend their own square, their own castle, and be ungrateful for where they were at. That night after we did that gig in Brighton with The Vines, everyone was really ashamed of us, all the people who'd been bigging us up said we did some 20 minute jazz-fusion."

JAMES ENDEACOTT: "They did a gig at Cherry Jam which I think was the first time it was the four of them. James Oldham came and reviewed it, gave it a really great review. They were wild, absolutely wild and it was so exciting. There were a couple of gigs with The Strokes, they went down well but they were still finding their feet really, and then I got them on with The Vines at Brighton. I did it because I knew The Libertines would blow The Vines away. They did a set that went on for 45 minutes of which a good 25 was some sort of fucking 'Jazz Odyssey' [*referring to an infamous 'difficult' piece played by the fictitious Spinal Tap*]. It went on and on and people were just like, 'What the hell is this?' – I was thinking, 'What the

43

fuck have I done?' I was depressed for two days. They could be either the best live band you'd ever seen or the worst. I mean, there were times when they were shocking."

PETE: "I remember once Carl giving a grand and a half away to a tramp. I did the same. It was in Brick Lane, we came out of the bagel shop and there was a girl who, for about five minutes of her life in Newcastle or Sunderland, would have been extremely beautiful, had a *joie de vivre* and a bit of hope. But she'd had it raped out of her or injected into her and she asked for some change. Carl just gave her this envelope. It all went a bit strange, she started shouting, 'What the fuck are you doing?!' She couldn't understand what was going on. Then this fella came out of nowhere and said, 'What are you doing to her?' so I gave him 50 quid. Then I gave 800 to a tramp on the Charing Cross Road."

CARL: "It's quite possible I gave it out, yeah, 'cos we were very ruinous. Having never had that much money before we didn't have much conception of its worth, only its weight. Pete, very wisely, after we'd been told it was in the bank, got it out all at once and we ended up putting it in the fridge in £50 notes. When someone would come round with some, er, provisions, it was nice to get a fifty out of the fridge and press it against their face. People got wind of it and it diminished a lot quicker than it ought to have. There was a bit of silliness really. I got into every fad possible, buying the most absurd things – like one of those ridiculous metal guitars, for no reason, and never playing it. Pete would buy all manner of junk and call it 'comfort shopping'.

"It got a bit sad once it did all diminish. I came back to the flat and Pete was out, and I found the record contract was out on the table – this was the first hint of insurrection on Pete's part, the first sign of a rift in our union – I saw that the contract was out of the glass case we kept it in and carelessly left lying about, and I thought maybe Pete had been reminiscing, cherishing and pondering how far we had come. I went to pick it up and saw the back of it where my signature was and realised that it was sort of embossed. Then I found a cheque missing from the joint account cheque book, and he'd had himself a grand. Of course he was oblivious to being in the wrong when I approached him on this and made out that I was being a greedy fool. I've never brought that one up before, actually."

PETE: "Anyone whose sofa I'd ever kipped on, who I'd ever scrounged a spliff off came to live at our new place, The Albion Rooms, 112a Teesdale Street, Bethnal Green, in a giant Arcadian reverie that hasn't ended really.

"I remember going to choose the place to live together. The tension was there immediately deciding who was going to have which room. Sadly my energy and positivity was matched by Carl's paranoia and cautiousness. From a lad who'd never picked up a copy of the *NME* in his life, never been on the gig scene or anything like that to someone who was staggering in at four or five o'clock every morning with crowds of strangers, powdering his nose and that. I used to wind him up and call him a ligger."

ROGER SARGENT: "We got round to The Albion Rooms to take the first press shots at about 11.30 for a midday start. We had a key for some reason, me and Tony, to let ourselves in. They turned up about three hours late to their own house for their own photo-shoot! Obviously they'd had a party the night before at the flat, because they'd just been signed and there was *money* everywhere [*laughs*], and drug paraphernalia, wraps and powder smears all over the tables; it looked fantastic, but at the same time you didn't really want to sit down anywhere!

"It was a bit hit-and-miss, they weren't instantly easy to photograph. Within an hour the rivalry had started between Pete and Carl about who would be at the front and whatever. I wasn't sure what

I'd got so I insisted we do another shoot.

"The next time Pete had turned up with these guards' jackets which, I don't know whether it's true, but they said they'd nicked off a stall in Petticoat Lane or somewhere. I was sceptical at first because I'm old enough to remember Menswear, but as soon as they put them on, they looked fantastic. I really didn't want this band being thought of as the new Menswear, which was quite possible, but that got completely bypassed – nobody even mentioned that but still nobody wanted to use those pictures. It was only when we were running out of shots and Europe needed some pictures that it turned up on the cover of German *Rolling Stone*. Then it got used on a poster that went around America and suddenly it was everywhere. We hadn't contrived to make an iconoclastic image – I didn't even want to shoot it!"

CARL: "My great grandad was in a famous cigarette advert wearing one of those jackets and he looks like me in it, so it was a bit of family heritage and that's the reason I endorsed it. Also when we got to the photo-shoot I wanted something that stood out. Pete always tries to incorporate things into some sort of 'masterplan' but I think it was quite accidental, just haphazard."

PETE: "Those red ones, I nicked from Brick Lane market but I nicked a *beauty* from Portobello, with all the chain mail. Those jackets were something that stemmed from me and were begrudgingly allowed to pass, like a little gig that's not been sanctioned or insured or just a particular idea, a particular way of life, and then all of a sudden it gets attributed to the band and then it's like, 'Oh yeah, *great*.'

"We went in and demoed 17 songs over two weeks, it was incredible – looping drums, and even Carl playing a bit of drums. Gary came in and did a few bits and bobs. While we were doing that, this big-nosed fella in a parka turned up; Adidas sambas he had on. It was Bernard Butler. 'What A Waster' was the common choice for the single, though I'd have released anything. James Endeacott said he was going to take out a full-page advert in the *NME* with just the lyrics to 'What A Waster'. I thought it was the greatest idea I'd ever heard."

JAMES ENDEACOTT: "For me it had to be 'What A Waster', we knew it would get no radio play but it was a total statement of intent. We were thinking about who was going to produce them and as they were very much a London band, and very guitar-based, we thought of Bernard who had been in Suede who, before The Libertines, had probably been the last, really big London band; maybe Blur you could count as well. Bernard was a big Smiths fan and he could really see The Smiths' element to it. Pete's a really big Smiths fan. For about the first year and a half I knew him, we used to send texts to each other – I would text him a line from a Smiths song and he used to reply back with the next line, but we'd *never* mention it when we'd see each other. We just had this silly game going on. It would happen at the maddest times as well, like at two in the morning, I'd get a text with 'Hang the DJ' or something!

"So we asked Bernard in and he just got in there and did it, but the band didn't really like the mix that he had done. We called a meeting, sat down with Bernard, got the mix sorted out and every-one was really happy with it. I think it did a job, it got the name out there and it got people excited. It was a really happy time, they really enjoyed being at RAK Studios [in St. John's Wood]. Mickie Most was alive still and he was around, and the fact that Bernard was involved was a really big thing for them at the time. And of course everyone loved the fact we were releasing a single with the word 'cunt' in it."

CARL: "In the classic tradition of icons and The Libertines, of course, I didn't have a clue who he was. He came to our demo sessions at Nomis and I thought he was a sulky kid in a parka sitting outside. Then Pete took me aside and filled me in with all these accolades as I think he was quite a big fan at the time. He was all right, seemed to be into it although we'd never had a producer before anyway so we were quite sort of subordinate at the start in that he had his role and he knew about it and we knew nothing about it really. Obviously we weren't going to sell ourselves short in any way, shape or form but I think he did us a good job, and we enjoyed the process. Later on down the line, personalities clashed and he and Peter just started bickering a lot. Bernard's method was, he's got a plan and you fall in with that plan but with Pete's mentality that's not going to happen."

PETE: "I can remember sitting down and grilling Bernard. I was having a bit of a headfuck at the time about fame and this monster that was gathering pace. I was asking, 'What's it like having people sing your songs back at you?', 'What's it like having people turning up to your gigs?', 'Do you have the same people turning up to your gigs?' and he'd say, 'I just laughed at it all, found it all funny.' I was uncomfortable from the start recording 'What A Waster', didn't like the vocals, couldn't listen back to it. I knew there's no way that man is gonna do the album with us – I couldn't imagine anyone doing it. All I can say, really, honestly and with any clarity is Mick Jones is a libertine and Bernard Butler isn't. Mick makes you want to go in to the studio and record your songs. The other fella made me want to sit in a cupboard and smoke crack. I threatened to knock him out a few times.

"It turns out, listening to it now, we made a fucking great debut single. Especially 'I Get Along'. The sound of it is quite unique, quite inspiring but I remember really sad, lonely mornings sitting alone in Bethnal Green listening to the opening bars of 'What A Waster' and having to take the needle off the record. I didn't think it was what we were about. We were putting it out to the world and I just felt powerless, but I let it go and just rolled with it. I realised then we were being presented as this fucking punk rock revival but in my heart the punk rock revival was dead on arrival, just another example of an artificial stimulant in the vein.

"Bernard Butler made it feel like a nine to five thing which I couldn't do. It went on and on and on and on. We were being dressed up wrongly. Taking the balls out of it? Having the balls painted different colours, when you should just let them hang as they are. He didn't really turn me on. He just wanted us to come past on the conveyor belt, he wasn't interested in getting to know us. I went round his house once and there was definitely something awkward about it.

"I don't think I connected with the people I was trying to reach. I preferred the demo. It was in the Top 40 for about two minutes, it was more a cult thing. We recorded it at RAK and mixed it in Shoreditch at the Strongrooms which was handy as we were practically living at the 333 club at the time; Mairead was working there. I remember long lazy cocktail afternoons, dancing all night, fucking everything in sight."

The *NME* wasted no time in making The Libertines cover stars,* showing the band cavorting with a Union Jack in regulation skinny leather jackets and ripped jeans, and Pete in a rare England World Cup '82 football shirt. If I hadn't known them anyway I'd have been attracted instantly. It was all there; the barnets, the clobber, the tunes, and an implied anarchy that you weren't getting from any contemporary bands I could think of. Interestingly, where Morrissey had been slaughtered in the music press for posing with the national flag 10 years earlier, these kids appeared to have reclaimed it,

---

* The *NME* like to claim that they were early champions of the band but, in terms of career progress, other bands, e.g. The Strokes, were featured on the paper's cover far earlier. I therefore feel it's wrong to say that they were behind The Libertines from Day One.

coming on like prime Who, unlike the ham-fisted mock-patriotic posture-fest of Blur back in the Britpop wars.

In the accompanying interview the band alluded to time served as rent-boys, tall tales of brothels and cat food poured on heads, geriatric drummers and civil disorder. A homoerotic overtone between Pete and Carl was played up, and I thought this gender-blurring added an exciting frisson to the whole package. Not for them any naff pseudo-Oasis swaggering, this ambiguity was refreshing. After all it didn't do Iggy or Bowie any harm. Even if you still took some convincing that this band were going to be special, that inaugural *NME* certainly set their stall out. They seemed naturals . . .

ROGER SARGENT: "Shooting that first *NME* cover was when we really started to sense that Pete and Carl were really competing with each other. It got to the point where they were competing with each other as to who would turn up the most late. They'd independently ring and say, 'Is Carl *there yet?*' 'No, no, he's not here yet,' and then Carl would ring, 'Is *Pete* there yet?' and then they'd turn up within 30 seconds of each other!"

TONY LINKIN: "Pete and Carl turned up so late that everyone was worried they weren't going to make it to the photo-shoot. Banny brought in the Union Jack, and Pete fell asleep on it and spilled red wine all over it. She'd only hired it and was really worried about taking it back!

"That first cover did come quite early, but it was the Jubilee week and they wanted a British band. 'What A Waster' was out – a brilliant single which obviously couldn't get any radio play to speak of. The band that was supposed to be on the cover was Fischerspooner, we bumped them off. A lot of people didn't like the idea they were on the cover of the *NME*, they were like, 'Where the fuck have they come from?', but they had been around quite a long time, it wasn't like they came out of nowhere. Pete and Carl had been working toward getting somewhere for a long time but a lot of people hadn't been giving them the time of day. Rough Trade was the only label that would actually go near them."

JAMES ENDEACOTT: "They were on the cover the week before the single came out which was unheard of. There was the real worry of, 'Is it going to be too much too soon?' and people were saying, 'It's too early for the first front cover,' but I was really adamant. I'd say, 'No, there's so much more to come, we're totally gonna justify this.'"

PETE: "It was a buzz, you can't knock it. Carl was blaming me for him being in the background, said it was my fault. In his mind it was like a plot, but to me it was just him putting his wedge [haircut] there which I didn't think was the way to represent the band. He had this paranoia about what they wrote about who."

CARL: "Yeah that [photo session] was exciting; we were in a studio and there were people you could ask to go and bring you stuff and they would. I was asking for about nine coffees that I didn't need and all that rubbish. Having the *NME* cover was a big deal and quite scary as well. Tony, our press officer, said to me, 'It's all gonna change after this, people are gonna stop you in the street, it'll never be the same again.' I was, like, 'Really? Wow.' And then nothing changed [*laughs*]. But, yeah, it was a big deal. I had a double chin though."

TONY LINKIN: "We did [the interview] on Mayday in the old Dive Bar in Soho while the riots were going on. They tried dragging James Oldham off to the riots afterwards, *as you do*. It was the second time I'd met Carl and he tried picking me up and dropping me down the toilet which is one of the things he likes to do:

I've been picked up and my pockets emptied in the centre of Nottingham, dropped on my head in Spain . . ."

It was all very exciting and it turned me on right from the start. I was too young for The Clash but when Manic Street Preachers arrived I felt I'd discovered 'my' Clash, a band to really believe in. Likewise, I'd been fleetingly enamoured with These Animal Men who seemed to have the whole package: tunes, attitude and looks but neither of those bands delivered on their early promise, at least not for me anyway. The Libertines arrived and I thought, "Third time lucky?" Now I was older, I'd stopped looking for "my" Clash but I felt sure that a whole generation were going to feel that that "special" band had finally arrived. It was odds-on that The Libertines were going to have an almost Smiths-like impact and mean a lot to kids of all ages.

It was definitely the first time since the Manics that a band would reach out and really connect with a young, disaffected audience. In time we'd find out the inner turmoil of The Libertines was every bit as dark and complex as Richey-era Manics but the crucial difference is where their slash-and-burn fatalism made cutting your arms up with a razor acceptable, The Libertines would be a steadying, life-affirming influence on their fans. Substitute "when I cut myself I feel closer to Richey" for "they're the best band in the world and they make my shit life feel special."

CHAPTER 4

Tell Me, What Can You Want Now You've Got It All?

IN 2002, the band I was in, Kill City, were putting out an EP with a low-budget video to accompany it. Our singer, Lisa Moorish, had become acquainted with Pete and Carl and asked if we could shoot it in their house, the now-legendary Albion Rooms. I think Pete learned of my involvement and okayed it. It was a long day with the basic storyboard of the video being the band frolicking with a gaggle of "lovelies", i.e. any good-looking birds we knew to make us look cool and decadent. Mairead and Tabitha were involved, who have since found considerable notoriety as The Queens of Noize. Carl was there for a while and I remember thinking it odd that he left the house in a big coat and scarf as it was the middle of July. Although he must have been roasting, he was already looking every inch the star.

I would be seeing a lot more of The Albion Rooms thanks to the generosity of both Carl and Pete. My marriage was going down the pan fast and I'd been turfed out of the conjugal bed. On learning this, they immediately offered to put me up while I got myself sorted. The band were going to Holland for a few dates and I could make myself at home. Situated in the grimy Bethnal Green backstreets as pounded by the band in the 'Up The Bracket' video, The Albion Rooms was a shrine to Pete and Carl's idiosyncrasies: an ostentatious spiral staircase, permanently pulled heavy curtains and a huge fish-eye mirror lent the gaff a Sixties cinematic feel. Pete's bed was like an assault course, three or four mattresses with unruly springs piled on top of each other, most of his wardrobe spread across it and an ornate brass headrail. There were parties most nights and watching the sun come up in a room full of wasted young women lent an air of *Performance* to the proceedings. On the down-side the place stank to high heaven and was so messy the mice had moved out in protest.

I'll never forget my first night when I was awoken by the sound of a ruckus directly outside Pete's bedroom window. A local youth was trying to do a runner from a cab and the elderly driver had got out and locked him in. The kid wanted out, and I watched in horror as he booted his way out of the passenger window and proceeded to give the poor bloke a savage beating. By the time I'd pulled my trousers on and got a bit of wood in my hand he was away. Nice place, you got here guys!

My being in residence must have been a blessed relief for the neighbour, a German woman who was quite possibly odder than Pete and Carl put together. She called the cops at the slightest provocation and on one occasion took the law into her own hands by storming round brandishing a small axe. Life *chez* Albion Rooms was so anarchic it made *Animal House* look like *The Good Life*. By the time Pete and Carl had vacated, the building was in a state of serious disrepair. All basic amenities had been cut off and the toilet had long since seen any action, or at least any action it could dispose of effectively.

PETE: "We called her [the neighbour] 'Vizzels', because she said that's what her budgie did whenever we played loud music [*adopts stern Teutonic accent*] – 'he *vizzels*!' She looked like a dog, like a pit-bull. She came around with a hammer and a chair leg. We got on quite well at first because I'm the kind of person, or *was* the kind of person, that would sit and listen to someone even if they were boring the arse off me; you just drift away and nod occasionally, and I did that with her but it was foolish because the things she was coming out with aren't the sort of things you want to be nodding along to: 'I *vill* not tolerate gaps in *ze* door of my mind whereby I stay for one month without saying *anyzing* to *anybody* . . . Alone . . . No noise . . . NEIN!!' "

From around this time on, Kill City and The Libertines became inextricably linked. Old friendships between myself and our guitar player Tom with John Hassall were renewed, Pete and Lisa had a little thing going, and in Pete, I found a kindred, if somewhat dangerous, spirit. He was totally fascinated when I told him I'd played schoolboy football with a kid called Karl Ready, who went on to play for his beloved QPR. To this day I'm still unsure if he believes me or not.

I learnt Pete had written a football fanzine in his teens – uncanny since I had earned the distinction of being the youngest fanzine writer in the country at 15 after penning my own magazine based around my home team Swansea, subsequently earning myself a debenture at *The Sunday Times* at 16. I didn't accept as it would have meant moving to London. I'd heard horror stories about the big bad smoke. Five years later, rock and roll had come into my life, making me forget the dream of being a sports journalist by relocating to London.

It was around this time (early 2002) that I really started to rate The Libertines as the proverbial dog's bollocks. One Sunday, in the early stages of our friendship, Pete invited me down to Nomis Studios in West London where he and Carl were mixing some tracks which would see the light of day as B-sides, bonus tracks and the like. Remember, all I'd heard of the band to this point was the 'What A

Waster' single and while that convinced me that they could cut the mustard in the "punky" genre they'd been cast in, I couldn't help but wonder if they were a one-trick pony, albeit a clever one. I jumped at the chance to visit Nomis as I'd heard it had been used by Paul Weller during his Jam and Style Council heyday. As it turned out, there wasn't much to see but as I entered the control room, my ears were met by the most beguiling music. Smooth and smoky, it had an almost supper-jazz vibe with a double bass used to great effect. "Who the fuck is this?" I enquired. Carl, who up to this point had been eyeing me with suspicion as I was Pete's "new" mate, replied, "It's us, innit."

You could have knocked me down. To this day I don't know what the track was but it demonstrated a depth and maturity that was light years ahead of their predictable, clod-hopping contemporaries. I suppose the closest comparison would be The Coral on a good day, but even then that would be too self-consciously psychedelic for its own good. I was genuinely impressed, thinking we've not heard the half of this band yet.

I recall a documentary I had watched some years earlier about the late, great Steve Marriott. Contained within it was a quote from Lionel Bart, who, in the late Fifties, had cast Marriott as The Artful Dodger in *Oliver!* Bart believed that had Marriott not died prematurely at a tragically young age he had the potential to go on to write musicals or songs for stage shows, leaving behind the rock template that had made his name. When I heard this mystery track at Nomis, I realised that spunky new-wave anthems are just the tip of the iceberg in terms of The Libertines' capabilities. If Bart were alive today I'm sure he'd say the same of Doherty and Barât. With their innate theatricality and poetry, they could certainly both pass as Artful Dodgers!

I enjoyed it when Pete would occasionally crash at my flat in Tower Bridge, where we'd sit up all night watching music films and videos. We watched The Sex Pistols' *The Filth And The Fury*

THE LiBERTiNes

The boys in the band, left to right: Carl Barat, John Hassall,
Pete Doherty and Gary Powell. *(Statia Molewski/Retna)*

A flyer for an early gig.
(Pete Welsh Collection)

Carl, John and Pete performing at Filthy McNasty's, July 2000.
(Pete Welsh Collection)

Carl and Pete at their flat in East London, August 2001.
(Lula Camus/Retna)

Rehearsing in Old Street, February 2002. *(Lula Camus/Retna)*

On stage at Crystal Palace, supporting The Sex Pistols,
July 2002. *(Sarahphotogirl/Retna)*

Carl with manager Banny Poostchi, Japan, summer 2002.
(Pete Welsh Collection)

Pete with fans in Sapporo, 2002, before doing a runner from the restaurant...
No, really. *(Pete Welsh Collection).*

In the EMI offices, Tokyo, summer 2002.
(Pete Welsh Collection)

Carl and John face the press in Spain, summer 2002.
(Pete Welsh Collection)

'Scarborough' Steve and Carl sozzled in the Albion Rooms, 2002.
(Pete Welsh Collection)

Carl and Lisa at RAK Studios, July 2002. *(Pete Welsh Collection)*

Pete on stage at Reading Festival, August 2002.
(Richard Skidmore/Rex Features)

Carl and Pete in a variation of the 'Up The Bracket' back cover. *(Pete Welsh Collection)*

Pete in drag for an HMV in-store appearance, October 2002. *(Stuart Mostyn/Redferns)*

At the end of the 'Up The Bracket' tour.
(Chris Daly)

Wet 'n' wild in Valencia, Spain, December 2002.
(Pete Welsh Collection)

In Valencia, December 2002.
(Pete Welsh Collection)

and Don Letts' Clash flick *Westway To The World*. I'd want to sleep but a wide-eyed Pete would insist we watched everything. Naturally I couldn't resist as it was great to turn him on to stuff he hadn't seen before. He was hungry to absorb the great legacies of these bands and I like to think I educated him with regard to my all-time favourite band, The Clash, so though it made me bleary-eyed and exhausted, it was fulfilling.

Pete invited me to Mickie Most's RAK Studios in St. John's Wood where The Libertines were recording their debut album *Up The Bracket*, with Mick Jones of The Clash at the controls. Since his post-Clash project Big Audio Dynamite had fizzled out in the mid-Nineties, not much had been seen or heard of Mick, even by eagle-eyed Clash obsessives like myself. He seemed a virtual recluse, surfacing occasionally to DJ at hip-hop and freakbeat nights. It seemed he had laid down his axe for good, and I knew it would take something special to tempt him back into the conventional guitar band fold. When I heard he was working with The Libertines I was thrilled for them but also thought, "About time too!"

JAMES ENDEACOTT: "We wanted Bernard to do the album because we liked the job he'd done on the single but he was not available, so Jeanette and I were talking one day in the office and she said, 'What about Mick Jones?' Jeanette knew The Clash from back in the day, she was sort of part of their crew, used to go out with Don Letts and she knew them really well. Again it was a London thing. We gave Mick a load of demos and he really loved them, so next I took Mick up to The Depot in Camden, where they were rehearsing, to meet them. They didn't really know anything about The Clash, and that's another thing I really like about The Libertines – their complete naivety about music and history of music. You realised it was pure and original and not contrived.

"We got there and Carl, John and Gary were there but no Pete, so I introduced them to Mick, and all of a sudden the door to the

57

studio burst open and Pete comes in on this old, battered-up scooter with loads of cans of beer! We just sat down, Mick skinned up, they played a couple of songs and Mick was dancing around with a beer in his hand and we all just got on really well. Mick was really up for doing it, so we went back to RAK and they were really, really great sessions, the band were there the whole time, it was really loose. Mick's style of production is basically, 'Let the band play, and I'm just going to tape it all and when there's a great take, that's the one,' so it was really organic and really live. There were a lot of late nights and a lot of craziness going on but everyone was really up for it."

PETE: "It was more of a personal thing you know. It was a wonderful introduction to this mythological world. You didn't even know if these people existed, *The Clash*, it was just some magical words. It's the sort of thing people carve into their chest, it meant something. It was almost a relief. It was like, 'At last, someone *to learn from*.' Someone who was going to really *let us in*. With Bernard he almost made you feel like you were trying to pick a fight, or trying to be *clever*, now with Mick he could see the innocence in you. You could sit at his feet and listen to stories about The Clash. We didn't know that much about The Clash and we learnt so much. Something as simple as [Mick] giving Carl a DVD, and Carl really treasured that, still does. He really appreciated it, and *watched* it an' all."

CARL: "I was expecting some sort of . . . well, whenever I thought of punk, I thought of some aggressive, crass-type figure spitting at us, saying, 'You aren't punk, you bunch of little fuckers,' and then fucking off and I wasn't too enamoured by that really, I didn't want that. I heard he was from The Clash, that was it, and I only knew two songs of The Clash. I was aware that it was a legacy to respect all the same. So he comes in, this slight man, very elegant, well-dressed, very charming and softly spoken and completely not what I'd expected at all. He came in with a bunch of cans, sat on the sofa and offered them around, listened to what we had, got up and had a little dance, skinned up a couple, said, 'Can you do that again?' So we do it again, looked up and he's asleep on the sofa all curled up. He was the nicest fella you could hope to meet, caring and clever, patient, just one of the boys, no overshadowing, looming figure which is what I didn't want because it wouldn't have worked with us. That's why we hit it off. With Bernard it was like the master and the pupils, although I've still got the greatest respect for him too."

Naturally I was like a kid in a sweetshop and spent a few balmy days in the studio that summer while the band were knocking 'Death On The Stairs' into shape, my personal favourite off *Up The Bracket*. I'd met Mick a few times previously through my good friend Steve Diggle but this was the first chance to spend quality time with the guy – watching him work and downing a beer or two. Pete knew this meant a lot to me and it was another example of his generous nature.

Mick is possessed of a gentle, dry wit and I saw some great examples of this. On one occasion, my mate (also called Mick) was at the studio, telling a story about a friend of his who had a predilection for crack cocaine and cheddar cheese. However he was allergic to the latter and while he could smoke crack "till the cows came home" he couldn't touch his favourite dairy product. On hearing this, Mick Jones, huddled over the control desk, turned around and nonchalantly remarked, "Swings and roundabouts, innit?" Priceless.

JAMES ENDEACOTT: "The last day of mixing at Whitfield Street, Mick brought in a copy of *The Guardian*. There had been some rioting in Argentina and there was a great picture of these riot cops. Mick just showed it to the band and said, 'This is the cover.' I mean, it's such a Clash cover. Mick loved the picture, and I think we had to pay three or four grand for the usage of it, but that's how that came about. I remember the first time we heard the mix of 'Up The Bracket' which would be the next single, me and Geoff and Jeanette were like 'Wow!' It was like we'd been hit by a fucking bolt, it was so much better than we were ever imagining."

PETE: "It was dreamlike, a lot of the songs weren't quite structured so it was a case of playing them again and again and they'd fall into place. But it wasn't a particularly happy time, it was very frustrating. I was *completely* wrapped up in the songs and particularly the words, how people were going to interpret the words, and how important it was to get it right. I was being so aware of myself and how I was seen by others. I was in a lather – I was seeing too many girls, I was doing too many drugs. Carl was completely out of his mind, he started using crack and heroin then when we were doing the first album, thought it was a big joke. We wrote a song called 'Skag And Bone Man' out of it, know what I mean? No one kicked *him* out of the band for it. He'd come in some days and he'd be completely incoherent, literally falling through the door. Gary and John were separate but me, Carl and Mick were on a mission.

"After a while it dawned on me that it was a bit of a nine to five, particularly for Gary and John and the engineer, and, to a certain extent, Mick as well, though it did loosen up towards the end and we'd stay late and spend a lot of time there. But mostly it was like, 'Be there at this time, go home at that time,' whereas for me, I could have *lived there* and that would be my life rather than clocking in and clocking out."

CARL: "They were good days. We'd turn up at a leisurely time, go through a few takes, break for dinner and for Mick to watch *EastEnders*, and be back in the studio until the small hours. It was quite affable and amicable, with a chain of people coming through to have a look at Mick Jones. I had one night on the skag and bone, courtesy of old Wolfie. We were waiting for what he promised as bugle to arrive, then marching through the rain at about four in the morning for a wee supply of bugle in Bethnal Green and finally some bird appears in a car. It came in the corner of a carrier bag, not a wrap, and it was bugle that you couldn't cut and you had to smoke and so I'd been waiting for it for so long I just smoked it. I turned up at the studio the next day *ruined* having not slept and was really pissed off. Then we were in the middle of a take of 'Radio America' and Danny Goffey [from Supergrass] came running into the studio in a pair of green tights, then disappeared again and I thought this is all getting far too surreal. At the end of the song I fell forward and smashed my head on the mic.

"'The Good Old Days', I loved recording that. We got hundreds of people in to sing the 'row-row-rows' – even Endeacott's on that somewhere. You can't hear him, luckily."

PETE: "'Skag And Bone Man' stands out because we wrote and recorded it all in a day. Just being able to take what was around me, all my feelings, all my emotions about everything and put it into a song, whip the band into shape and give Carl his little 30 seconds for his solo and just BANG! It was there and I was happy, I was proud.

"I was playing my own sort of long, psychological card game of fame and this was when I started using the internet as well actually, nipping upstairs at RAK, and being absolutely amazed that someone would be moved enough to go on the internet saying that they liked this band The Libertines. I think I was, and maybe still am, the biggest Libertines fan around and it was great to meet like-minded people."

Mick Jones' involvement with The Libertines cemented a relationship that seemed God-given. Bernard Butler did a decent job of the first single but Mick had a better understanding of where the band

61

were coming from, and had enough of a presence to keep them in some kind of line.* While it's easy to trace the lineage from The Clash to the Libs, it may surprise many to learn that neither Pete nor Carl were particularly *au fait* with the Westway wonders. In fact I don't even think they knew who Mick Jones was before Rough Trade drafted him in to produce the demos.

At the time *Up The Bracket* was released, some called into question Jones' elementary style of production. Two years down the line his work stands up nicely, borne out by his use of similar methods on *The Libertines*. His no-frills hands-off style is what captures their true sound. As well as the obviously productive working union, I've witnessed a lot of affection passing three-ways between Mick, Pete and Carl. Indeed Carl attributes a lot of the credit for keeping the band going during the fractious, second album sessions to Jones.

Sadly, not long after the release of *Up The Bracket*, Mick's old compadre Joe Strummer died in December 2002. Only the night before, I'd spoken to Mick at The Barfly where he was DJ'ing with his old mate Tony James as part of The Queens of Noize Xmas party. He was in fine spirits, now back on form thanks to his work with The Libertines.

When the news broke that Joe had passed away it didn't really sink in for a few hours; not that I knew him, though I did meet him a couple of times and he was everything you'd expect – gracious, attentive, warm, a *brilliant* guy. My thoughts soon turned to Mick and how he was dealing with it. The fact that it was three days before Christmas exacerbated the tragedy. I happened to see Mick a month or so later and I offered my condolences. He told me how glad he was that he'd accepted Joe's invitation to play a few Clash numbers onstage at Acton Town Hall (November 2002) for a

---

* Unfortunately, Butler was one of only a few people who I couldn't persuade to talk to me for this book.

Firemen's benefit in what turned out to be his last London show. Mick told me, "I almost didn't do it, you know."

The Libertines were asked in foreign press interviews for their thoughts but Pete and Carl respectfully explained that they'd never met Joe and weren't in a position to comment. A year later, on the anniversary of Strummer's untimely death, Pete was the first person I enlisted to perform at a packed tribute night at Filthy McNasty's, the profits going to Joe's tree-planting charity. MC was Jock Scot, a pub poet who moves in the same circles as Pete's Filthy's bunch and had served time as a Clash roadie, so his credentials brought a much-needed air of authenticity to the proceedings. It was Jock who entertained the restless hordes while I sweated to get Pete down to the pub. The errant headliner eventually turned up some two hours late, post-curfew, and performed 'I Fought The Law', 'Jail Guitar Doors' (oh, the irony), 'Remote Control' and a clutch of his own stuff. Everything had gone full circle from that first moment I heard The Clash and fell in love, to getting to know Mick, to getting my mates involved to raise money for Joe's cause. It felt good.

The Libertines were getting better gigs and I was fortunate enough to attend almost every show they played that summer. When I heard they were supporting The Sex Pistols at Crystal Palace in July, Pete left passes at the gate for me and Lisa. We arrived late and didn't see or hear a note of their set but in retrospect I wasn't bothered. Apparently, the band hadn't gone down too well on a bill that included a load of crusty Levellers-style bands, singing about cider, squatting and whatever else to an ageing, boorish punk crowd.

The Pistols themselves were a shadow of the band I'd seen perform six years earlier at Finsbury Park. John Lydon was just tedious, ranting between songs about everything from Tony Blair to David Beckham. That the once-mighty Pistols crown was to be claimed by their lowly support band was somewhat ironic.

ROGER SARGENT: "Pete had a little old-school Sony tape recorder with him and he'd recorded something John Lydon had said backstage and then proceeded to play it through his mic out onstage. They got stuff chucked at them as soon as they walked on. I remember Pete got a can chucked at him and it hit him right in the face. He picked it up, squeezed it, and drank the contents – fuck knows what was in it, but it was like, fuck *you*! He was blowing kisses to all the people who were shouting at him as he was walking offstage, and I remember him throwing his guards jacket into the crowd. Carl threw his but it didn't quite make it and it landed in the pit."

PETE: "Oh fucking hell, the Pistols was absolute fantasy, I was just playing repeats of the *Steptoe And Son* theme music on my little tape recorder, knowing that he was next door in this little prefabricated dressing room, and a recording of an interview with him [*imitates Lydon*]. 'Is it because we're working class, you expect us to stay in our scummy little council estate? Fuck off! What about all these trashy little pop stars you've got running about left, right and centre? I don't hear you bitching about *them bum'oles*!'

"John said to him, 'Are you gonna catch any of our set today?' and he replied, 'I don't miss a trick,' and then he was shouting at Mairead, 'You *bloody Spice Girl*, you've got no manners!' She was going, 'Oi Lydon, lend us a quid?' The only thing I remember about the actual set was being hit by a can of Heineken. I've still got a little bump actually where it chipped my skull, but [*mock serious*] I don't like to talk about it.

"I bumped into Lydon. I was knocking about with Tabitha at the after-show party. We got ourselves a couple of drinks and tucked ourselves away in this little alcove for a kissy-kissy and he bowled over and said, 'These seats are reserved for *us*, *be fair*!" and that was it. But I felt also throughout the night, maybe I was imagining it, there was something going on, we were clocking each other

64

without saying anything. A fairly intimidating character I think it's safe to say but Jeanette, who works for Rough Trade and was in PiL, apparently is the one person in the world who he doesn't talk down to and makes an effort to be pleasant to. So one of these days I'm gonna get around to getting Jeanette to take me to meet him."

The band were earning rave reviews with incendiary shows at venues like London's ICA and Cherry Jam, but at Crystal Palace they were finding the transition to the bigger stage a little problematic.

TONY LINKIN: "They played the Reading Festival [August 2002] which was a disaster, an absolute disaster where everything went wrong. I saw them the night before, warming up in Chelmsford and they'd been brilliant but at Reading the equipment just fucked up. Carl's amp fucked up on the very first song. Everyone was there to see them and everyone walked away thinking they were rubbish – it set them back so much. A lot of people have always doubted this band and that was just another reason to doubt them."

PETE: "Carl's amp blew up which gave me an opportunity to try out 'The Ha-Ha Wall' for the first time with just Gary and John who knew it. It's another sore point in a way because Carl never really had a part for it – I suppose he's learned my part for it now [*sarcastically*]. At that stage we were playing to very apathetic crowds, where you'd have maybe a tenth of the crowd would know how to have a good time and the rest of them would be arms-folded, 'What are you lot about then?' which I never understood, that mentality. We rolled offstage at Reading fighting and similarly by the time we got to Leeds we had a proper fisticuffs. Amidst all this I saw Carl – this very, very unhappy boy and I went to put my arm around him, literally to say, 'Are you all right?' and he's gone, 'Fuck off!' and pushed me away and for the first time I stood up to him. It had always been taken for granted that he was harder than me, and he was, but I lost it that day. It was a glimpse of what was to come. I stood up to him and I couldn't be hurt any more. It was the beginning of the end then, I think, we were drifting apart. We were splitting apart onstage. I was finding I couldn't bear it, couldn't bear that hurt. Just complete loneliness knowing he wasn't there for me."

CARL: "Reading was just embarrassing. My amp blew on the first song and I was stuck there like a turkey. For the first time ever, my entire family were there in the audience and yeah, it was quite upsetting really. It went on pretty much without a hitch after that. I was really pissed off with Pete as we came offstage as I felt he was always trying to upstage me, like kick me up the arse when I bent over and try and make me look like a comedy puppet. It was *my* big dream to be playing this place as well, so I thought that was really inappropriate. I raised it afterwards and he obviously assumed that I was intending violence, so he started throwing punches at me and before I even knew that this situation was ensuing Gary was holding me back by my hair. This was at Leeds. At Reading, I remember going on to the tour bus with my old man to show him around and there just being clouds of smack everywhere. It wasn't the ideal situation."

JAMES ENDEACOTT: "I didn't go to the Reading gig, I went to the Leeds show the day after but I'd been getting reports about how bad Reading had been. At Leeds, they turned up and Pete and Carl were fast asleep until 20 minutes before they went on. They got onstage and I turned round to my wife after two songs and said, 'What the fuck is going on here?' They were dreadful. They came off, they had a big fight, Pete and Carl punched each other. Banny got really angry with them, John was sulking, Pete was almost in tears and Carl was just furious. It was an absolute nightmare. It was just a *bad* gig, they were all hungover and hadn't slept properly and they weren't really taking it that seriously."

In September 2002, Kill City joined the 'Up The Bracket' tour at Coventry for six dates. The previous week's *NME* had run a double-page live feature following The Libertines in Scotland and the pictures and report suggested they were inspiring scenes reminiscent of Beatlemania. Naturally we were excited to be a part of it. Kill City had only formed a few months earlier and, after signing to Poptones, we'd been lucky enough to bypass the obligatory Bull And Gate circuit and go straight on to supporting the hippest band of the moment at proper venues. We rolled up to the Coventry Colosseum in our splitter van and immediately I sensed something was wrong. The venue itself and surrounding area had to be the most bleak, run-down slag heap of a joint I'd ever seen; a large brick outhouse in the middle of a tenement-style council estate. Let's just say it was no Madison Square Garden.

Loading our gear inside we were barely greeted by either the Libs or their other support, Pete's mates Left Hand. The atmosphere could have been cut with a crash cymbal. Seemingly, everyone had got a bit overexcited the previous night in Leeds and there had been a flare-up, resulting in Pete's then-squeeze Tabitha copping a black eye, 'Scarborough' Steve (along for the ride) a thick lip, and one of Carl's brogues getting filled with piss. I felt for him as he loved those brogues.

Understandably, The Libertines and Left Hand were on a grunting level of communication, the latter sullenly skinning up in their carpet van while the former licked their wounds on the flash tour bus. We thought, 'Fuck this, we're out of here till show time,' and ventured into Coventry for some sanctuary. That was our second mistake. We hit a boozer that was packed full of football hooligans who took offence at our long hair, making us exit sharpish.

By the time the night was over all three bands had delivered blistering sets and, thus buoyed, kissed and made up. In fairness the crowd was one of the best we encountered and it was fun working on the merchandise stall, chatting up the female students, though I'll never forget how grim the actual environment was. Sent to Coventry? No thanks!

Over the course of those six nights we spent on the road with them, I became hooked on The Libertines. Each night after our set, I'd watch these young malcontents' skinny torsos ricochet and pogo violently about the stage. Being a fair bit older I wasn't sure if I should feel this way about a new band but I couldn't help it. They were that exciting.

PETE: "[That tour was] not a really happy time. The camera didn't lie, but you can laugh and joke and still be unhappy. We were battling so much with each other, and with the world. I don't want to eliminate the rest of the world, or eliminate the rest of my friends by saying mine and Carl's is some special, unique friendship. I'll look into anyone's eyes who I'm sharing that kind of performance with, those kinds of emotions with, those kinds of songs with. I'll look into anyone's eyes who I love and I believe in, it's not just Carl. People picked up on it because that's what we presented – 'Pete and Carl' – do you know what I mean? It's not a fallacy, but it's not exclusive to Carl; we're not *gods*. People have seen how solid it is, and people have seen how much the friendship means to him – fuck all.

"In the end I did have to stand shoulder-to-shoulder with Carl. I always will, but, yeah, Left Hand let themselves down, I think. It should have been an opportunity to travel and broaden the mind, not get their noses broadened by Northern bouncers, which is how it ended up. [Left Hand] are really talented but extremely volatile and their own worst enemies. What it was, they *really* upset Carl. They put curry powder and bananas in his shoes. Someone also drew swastikas all over 'Scarborough' Steve's face and wrote, 'I Am

A Queer,' and he didn't know about it and went walking around Manchester."

CARL: "It was gruelling but it was good, everything was still in our control then. I enjoyed that tour immensely. There was a lot of love, a lot of good times, and very few setbacks. A lot of bickering and a few moments but on the whole everything was in order. There was a lot of silliness and *Grange Hill*-antics with Left Hand. They filled one of my shoes with crap and cut the laces up, just tiresome really. There was some degree of argy-bargy but in the classic *Grange Hill* passing-the-buck situation, no one actually admitted to having done it."

Each night threw up fresh lunacy. In Bristol, we teamed up with another band we knew from London, The Beatings, who happened to be in town, and ended up seriously rat-arsed in a drum-and-bass club of all places. Carl and I got into some bother with the bouncers.

The next day, as we crossed the Severn Bridge into Wales, Libertines folklore recounts that I let out a deep primal groan to signal our entrance to the land of my fathers. Carl swears it was something to behold, but despite my moniker, I'm not particularly patriotic so it was probably just a burp that they characteristically romanticised. That night in Cardiff, I was on my way to the notorious docks area with a dog-rough lady-of-the-night when John and Gary happened upon me purely by chance and dragged me back to the hotel. When they told me the next morning, I didn't know what the hell they were talking about – I thought we were still in Bristol.

The following day the tour party remained in Cardiff before pressing on to Exeter. I used the opportunity to take a train to Swansea to watch my team. At the match, I was astonished to find a lot of my old friends popping copious amounts of ecstasy, a new phenomenon I was oblivious to, having left football behind nearly 10 years previously. Here I was, surrounded by some of the roughest, toughest hooligans, all nutted on pills which, at £1.50 a throw, were cheaper than a half-time pasty. Enlightened, I returned to Cardiff's Marriott Hotel where a high-spirited Pete and Lisa were ensconced in Pete's room, getting slaughtered on Vodka Martinis. It was a long night, the room service bill must have been astronomical as to save legwork we'd order a tray of nine vodka martinis at a time – three each.

I recounted this incredible tale of loved-up louts, of hooligans on ecstasy. Quick as a flash, Pete had his acoustic guitar and was bashing out an E chord (fittingly) and crowing, "Hoo-ooligans on E, meat pies and burberry!" There's a line about pilled-up hoolies, "not burying hatchets, we only carry melodies, to bury in your heads". It's a measure of Pete's compositional skills that he took subject matter that I would never have seriously considered and turned it into a credible tune.

A few weeks later, Pete was strolling around, minstrel-like, singing a completed version of 'Hooligans On E'. I was surprised as I thought it so throwaway it would have remained within the four walls of that hotel room. However it sounded good and proved a favourite when aired at the ill-fated Babyshambles gigs the following summer. It was around the time when Pete was in jail that I took the liberty of recording my own version of 'Hooligans On E' with Mick from Kill City, with a harder edge and a Strokes-y guitar line which differed greatly from Pete's version. Upon hearing it after his release, he was complimentary but insistent that his was the definitive version. I was disappointed as they were both good variations, but impressed that Pete had a steely belief in our original. Later on the track was recorded for the second Libertines album, but didn't make the final cut. I was a bit gutted that it fell by the wayside since Alan McGee liked it so much he wanted to release it as a single.

When the first album hit the shops at the end of September, the press appeared unanimous. There was barely a dissenting voice, although initial sales failed to match the acclaim it was met with.

"Genuine talent of indisputable class," said *MOJO*'s Pat Gilbert while *The Sunday Times* declared it "messier than chucking-out time at The Blind Beggar." For a record that was so elemental in its production and sonic impact it was receiving lofty analysis from various critics. Pete's "Lambeth Walk-isms" married to Carl's "Duane Eddy riffs" and the broad church of reference points gave them plenty to pore over. The band's art and literary pretensions, with nods to Oscar Wilde, William Blake, Tony Hancock and Francis Bacon, gave their profile considerably more gravitas than clumsy contemporaries like The Datsuns and their predictable, myopic AC/DC fixations or The Vines' third-rate grunge re-hash.

The Libertines' innate Englishness and celebration thereof appeared to be unconditionally embraced by the majority of the press. It was nearly 10 years since Blur had undergone a style overhaul with their 'British Image #1' which provided the catalyst for "Britpop". Whether you considered that a good or bad thing, it all looks rather cynical and manufactured with hindsight. If it's true that trends come around in seven or eight year cycles then The Libertines love of all-things-English seemed to land at the right time.

JAMES ENDEACOTT: "A lot of people were sort of disappointed with the record. A lot of people were disappointed with them live. The boys were telling stories and everybody thought they were just chancers, they were making it all up. At first people thought they were a joke, they didn't really take them that seriously. It was really disappointing how it sold, but it took people a long time to get it. When you work with a band you always want your mates and your peers to like it, and a lot of my friends didn't like it. I remember a gig at the 100 Club where [critic] Keith Cameron, who's opinion I respect, he didn't like them, but he went to that gig and he called me over after they'd played and went, 'You were right,' and for a good six months after the album came out, I'd have friends coming up, saying, 'Oh James, you were right about The

Libertines.' But people were jealous of their looks, the way they were, the fact they were so natural."

The band's reputation for madcap antics and excess was largely cultivated on that autumn 2002 tour. A disbelieving *NME* ran weekly bulletins about bad behaviour, the likes of which hadn't been seen since Oasis. In reality it was pretty run-of-the-mill stuff, just what you'd expect from a bunch of kids let loose on the road for the first time.

As these were still early days, the tour operated on a limited budget. That meant the tour manager would be responsible for just about everything: lifting, shifting and generally copping a load of earache from his charges. The poor unfortunate in this case, we'll call him 'X', was already at a disadvantage when we found out his previous occupation was a policeman. Chaos reigned from start to finish of that tour, pushing the poor chap to the limit. I felt for him really as he wasn't a bad bloke, and he had one hell of a job to do, being responsible for getting the band from A to B and onstage within an allotted time. It was a tricky brief even when working with nice boys like Coldplay or Keane, but with a bunch of reprobates like The Libertines, it was nigh on impossible.

Mistakenly, X tried to exert an almost paternal influence on the band and while John and Gary gave him little or no grief, Pete and, to a much lesser degree, Carl made his life a misery over the course of a 25-date tour. Pete's anti-authoritarian attitude was still in its infancy, far from being the total "Fuck you" insurgent he is today. His behaviour was more like the class rebel seeing how far he could push the teacher on a school trip. It was, however, the first time I'd seen Pete openly flex his enmity on someone, and it wasn't pretty.

When Kill City joined the tour, X quickly identified yours truly as the main mayhem instigator and was mightily relieved when we played our six dates and returned to London. He'd marked my card a few months earlier when the Libs supported The Sex Pistols at

Crystal Palace. After the show, Pete set about trashing the back-stage area for a laugh. I joined in, and the pair of us ended up pelting X with ice. He was huffing and puffing trying to restore order but he couldn't lay a hand on either of us as we baited him mercilessly. He ended up soaked. It was pure punk rock mischief, but I remember finding it odd that John Lydon, standing nearby with his ever-present gang of goons, frowned upon us. How times change, eh?

After a particularly nasty stand-off with Pete in Southampton, X was sacked by the band for simply being too strict. In turn, he told the *NME* that he'd never seen "drug-fuelled debauchery" like it in 22 years of working with bands.

ROGER SARGENT: "At the start of that tour, I flew up to Scot-land where it was commencing and, getting off the plane, there was a message on my phone from Hannah [Bays, band friend] in whis-pered tones saying, 'Roger, you've got to help us . . . we're stuck on the tour bus, we've been locked in for six hours,' and I was like, 'What the fuck, what's going on?' and I called her back. Pete had basically snuck her and three others into his room – he had his own little room on the tour bus, because the tour manager wasn't really allowing anybody on. They'd gone all the way up to Scotland and when they'd arrived he hadn't managed to get them out. Well, there's no ventilation, everyone was really hot – I mean, imagine being in Pete's room *anyway!*"

JAMES ENDEACOTT: "We got [X] in because he'd done The Strokes for us but they had sacked him because he was too rigid with them, he was too on time, he was almost too good at his job! He was exactly the same with The Libertines, but it was obvious that rigid organisation was not going to work with this band. Bands like to be late and he was just too much. He'd been with us to Japan and that was another nail in it for him.

"But that was fun that first Japanese trip. We did a festival called Summersonic and we got on really well with Mike Skinner from The Streets. In Osaka on the first night, me and Carl went to this bar and asked this bar-owner guy if he could get any drugs and he said no, but then twenty minutes later said, '*I can get some crystal meth?*' So we got it and we were with this guy and he took us to this lap-dancing club at about six in the morning, and there were girls coming down poles and picking up dollars in their fannies and what-have-you. They asked me and Carl if we wanted a private show but they were really tired and weren't really into it so we thought we'd be nice and said why don't we just go out, with these six pole dancers?

"We were in a bar and I was paying for everything with my credit card and they said, 'Mr Endeacott, there's a call for you,' and I was like, 'What? Seven in the morning in a bar in Japan?' and this voice says, 'Hello, this is First Direct bank in Leeds, we're noticing that your card has been used quite a lot in the last two hours in Osaka, we wonder if it's stolen?' I said, 'No, no it's fine, it's me.' Of course when I get back I realise I've spent nearly a grand. It was only afterwards I realised that these girls probably do this all the time, fleecing blokes dry [*laughs*].

"It was a really memorable time. We stayed in the Tokyo Hilton and one morning at eight o'clock there was a knock on my door, and Pete and Carl just ran in stinking of brandy and whiskey, obviously been up all night, and they'd bought a load of firecrackers. There was a bowl of fruit and they put firecrackers in oranges and apples which were exploding everywhere; then they went in my mini-bar and poured whiskey and vodka and brandy all over my bed, and tried to strip me, both out of their minds but it was really, really great fun. They absolutely wrecked my room, though."

TOBY McFARLANE (MUSICIAN): "I was in Japan with JJ72 and was warned about the groupies by a fan. I said I wasn't into that but what's she like anyway? [*Japanese accent*] 'She is very big boobs, she is Libertines wife when they are in Japan,' so I steered clear!"

PETE: "We'd been up all night, bombing around Tokyo, breaking into bars. We found this funny complex where the lifts went up to different bars and we found ourselves on this level where the bar was actually locked so we bust open the door and the pair of us stole bottles of gin and an umbrella. We realised it was all on CCTV and had to leg it. We had a couple of nights where we were inseparable, having a blast together and the rest of the time it was pure sadness and dislocation. There was one gig where I'd had enough and I tried to explain it to everyone but no one was really listening so I explained it differently: I took John's bass off him, put it through his amp, tore the drum kit apart, kicked Carl's amp over and they all walked offstage and left me.

"I ended up in a bar over the road with Carl while they put all the amps back together, and then me and Carl went back on with him on drums – Gary refused to carry on – then me on drums and Carl singing, it was madness. We ended up doing a couple of hours with different line-ups, and it ended with me, Carl, Gary and John with one guitar. From that moment on, though, it was clear that I didn't want Gary or John on bass or drums. I wanted to do an acoustic album, get a new line-up. I told them all. Gary pretended I wasn't saying it, I'd say, 'It's been great, you know, but I want to get it going different,' and he'd say [*adopts American accent*], 'Yeah, sure, it's up to us, we gotta make it,' and they all ran off to Banny, really. 'He can't do this.' Carl just wanted an easy life."

CARL: "There was a bit of silliness in Sapporo. We just fell out, I don't know whether it was cold turkey, or just depression, or boredom, but John started playing the bass while Pete was playing his guitar at the soundcheck and for the rest of the day he was in a stink and he did his classic, 'I'm gonna do something to remember at this gig, boys,' which just fills everybody with tired trepidation, and puts everybody on guard and just makes for bad energy all round. Two songs in, he fucked everything up so nothing worked any more and disappeared.

"Disappointedly I left the stage and waited a while, went to find him, took him over the road for a drink while the crowd were baying for blood, or music, or just something. Had a couple of shots of sake, made friends, said I wasn't angry with him, went back onstage, nothing worked except one guitar and we just tried to blag the rest of the show."

As the UK tour wrapped up in October, the second single, the title track from the forthcoming debut album *Up The Bracket*, was released as a double A-side with 'Boys In The Band'. *NME* made it Single of the Week, and it received blanket airplay from London station XFM, ram-raiding its way into the Top 20. The band played an anarchic session on Zoë Ball's drive-time show, where Carl made an obvious impression on the bubbly hostess as she didn't stop drooling on about him for weeks.

PETE: "I remember having a long discussion the night before that XFM session with Banny and Carl about, well, certainly Carl was a bit worried about the amount of coke he was taking, and we came to some sort of agreement that there would be no more cocaine while we were 'working' if you like – recording, and in particular, the next day at the radio it was fairly important we were gonna nail it down. I think within 10 or 15 minutes of being at XFM, the dealer was in the car park. It was a fucking *blizzard*.

"With *NME*, you see that you've got Single of the Week, and then you see that they've misquoted the lyrics. I don't know if they do it deliberately but it's one of those things that never fails to irritate or even demoralise, especially when they did it with 'What A Waster'. I really wanted someone to write about 'Up The Bracket':

'What a brilliant song, brilliantly crafted and sung by Peter Doherty' but it just became part of the myth of Doherty/Barat songwriting classics but that was a song that was so fucking dear to me from start to finish. I'd watched it grow like a little plant, sat in a basement in Dalston in those months before we got signed, listening to The La's and wanting to write a song like that."

The video, filmed in The Albion Rooms, aped the Kill City promo we'd shot in the same surroundings a couple of months earlier, even down to a bunch of girls jumping around with gay abandon (sound familiar?). These included London club faces Tabitha and Mairead, the DJ and designer Pam Hogg, and two peculiar twins who looked like they were from *The Addams Family*. A barnstorming performance on *Later With Jools Holland* did the single's cause no harm, neither did an observant Mick Jones' assertion that the dynamic between Doherty and Barat reminded him more of Lennon and McCartney, than his own with Joe Strummer. The band were receiving plaudits beyond their wildest dreams.

Around this time, The Libertines made their second appearance as *NME* cover stars on the October 19 issue. Up to this point interviews with the band, and Pete in particular, had portrayed him as cryptic, cosmic and downright silly, talking entertaining if somewhat tangential nonsense. Now the paper had decided to probe deeper into the darker heart of the band with a focus on its recreational habits. A photo-shoot showing them looking battle-scarred from the rigours of their first major tour was accompanied by startlingly candid admissions from Pete about his alleged heroin use.

Since rock'n'roll began, bands have taken drugs and this has often been the principle focus of much rock journalism. While the majority of musicians have experienced some level of drug abuse it's rare to find them coming right out with their narcotic preferences, especially if that happens to be heroin, the dirtiest and most socially unacceptable of the lot. The Velvet Underground wrote a song about it and the Heartbreakers clearly *looked* like they were using but their comments on the topic were largely ambiguous. In the Eighties and Nineties drone merchants, Spacemen 3 and spin-off Spiritualized, and the likes of Primal Scream often wore their drug addled hearts on their sleeves. It was no secret that the late Kurt Cobain and his femme fatale Courtney Love had used the drug, as had half of the grunge scene in the US.

It was also no secret that heroin had been around the London music scene ever since the late Sixties. The whole mid-Nineties' Britpop thing was fuelled by amphetamine sulphate and cocaine and certain individuals had made the natural progression to smack to deal with the comedown. Several members of Elastica were strongly rumoured to have succumbed, though, in their case, I couldn't help feeling it was as much of a fashion statement as anything else. A couple of the Menswear boys got into it and had a fair bit of bother getting out of it. A few years of heroin hell in exchange for 15 minutes of fame seems a raw deal to me.

With The Libertines' star firmly in the ascendant, here was their leader openly alluding to wanton chemical husbandry, seemingly without a damn for his own reputation, or the knock-on effect of such proclamations on his young fanbase. While I found this honesty refreshing and intriguing, I did question the wisdom of it.

PETE: "It frightened me that article. I looked like a doll in it, ugly. It wasn't a conscious decision but it was a huge error of judgement on my part. I'll say this now: that interview was like a therapy session, so much came out, so many good things came out, explanations for what I'd said about heroin, so many ideas I had about heroin, and British culture, and youth and growing up but of course none of it was printed. They just printed these parts and I felt really, really foolish. I was really looking forward to reading those arguments, it was quite a battle of wits between me and Carl but it wasn't presented like that. It was presented like we were just juvenile or without anything to say of any interest.

"The fella in question I vowed to do him over. It depends how important you see the *NME* as being. Personally I do get quite involved in even what's written in a fucking letter from someone from fucking Scunthorpe. I'm probably the wrong person to ask because I do actually believe that it's quite important what's said *but* I think most people are a bit more detached, and hopefully more intelligent than to be swayed by comments in the *NME*. I only had negative things to say about heroin."

In that same article, Pete gave an ominous portent of events that were to unfold over the next nine months when he remarked to Carl, "It's going to turn sour. I think it's going to turn sour and then we'll get back together. But you know as well as I do that we disagree on major issues."

If Pete had hinted that all was not shipshape and Bristol fashion aboard the Albion, Keith Cameron would be one step ahead of the game when he interviewed the band for the March 2003 edition of *MOJO*. Though the feature was playful enough, Cameron obviously sensed that the band's infrastructure was built on shifting sand, noting: "There is an hermetic tightness to The Libertines' realm, a blinkered worldview which shelters them from the pressure of being the new young saviours of rock, but which may eventually suffocate them due to a fatally diminished perspective," and how "[in the world of The Libertines], the future is unwritten." Hmm . . .

PETE: "That was no great foresight. It's only because we've *always* fallen out, and quite severely. Back when we were on the dole, or working in the theatre, we'd fall out and then that would be it. [Carl] would fuck off for a couple of months and everything would be at odds. I'd just be pressing on with the band on my own. This is how it ended up with me being exiled, the fact that I continued with the hermetic existence whereas Carl completely opened himself up to the outside world and to a different way of life, and therefore was seen as sort of the acceptable one, and was able to win the support of the infrastructure simply because he made himself more conventional. I don't mean that in a derogatory way, just in that people saw him more likely to get the job done."

I ran into the guys the day they gave that interview at Filthy McNasty's (where else?). Pete, especially, was well oiled and as I walked down Amwell Street with him he was unsteady on his feet, clutching a pint of Guinness. We were heading back to Wolfman's flat where he was staying at the time, when he suddenly hurled the pint glass high above his head, about 40 feet or so. It came down with an almighty crash, splintering glass everywhere. It could just as easily have come down on his bonce – or mine for that matter. I realised then, this kid really doesn't give a fuck.

Shortly after this, The Libertines supported Morrissey, one of Pete's idols, at Brixton Academy. Although the band gave what I considered to be a reasonable account of themselves, they still hadn't learned how to walk the walk on a stage of that size, and their short set seemed to go over the heads of Mozzer's notoriously prickly audience. A little over a year later they would be back on that same stage playing three sold-out nights back-to-back, as the consummate rock act.

PETE: "It wasn't easy to be honest. I seem to remember during 'Time For Heroes' something loosened up and we got a smattering of applause. Physically the connection with Morrissey was a bit jumbled because I put my hand out to shake his, and he put his hand out to do a sort of fist-clench, so I switched to the clench and he stopped the clenching and put his hand out. It was all over quite quickly and unsatisfactorily, it was quite muted, though I remember

Gary saying to him, 'Nice ring, where'd you get that?' and he said, 'Greece.' I think he prefers The Libertines without me, he went to see them in LA."

CARL: "He had a very big presence, but very few words. He had a whole section of the floor we weren't allowed to walk through, you had to go up then down to get to the stage rather than just walk along. He was always flanked by security guards but he seemed decent enough. I rate him as a great lyricist and I respect him for being true to himself. Can be a bit of a misery, though."*

Despite the lukewarm reception to their set, the band were intent on partying hard afterwards. I seem to remember even Gary was "bangled" to use his own peculiar vernacular. While the affable drummer was happy with the occasional booze bender, his erratic leader was developing a worrying taste for the hard stuff, as I witnessed for myself back at Wolfman's pad. Pete nonchalantly produced a rock of crack cocaine the size of a golf ball from his pocket and set about it heartily. Not for the first or, indeed, last time, I despaired of the guy.

JAMES ENDEACOTT: "I first noticed Pete getting a bit out of hand when we were doing the video for 'I Get Along' and he didn't show. He just didn't turn up and it was like 10, 12 grand down the drain. He just wasn't turning up to things, being a bit of a loose cannon and just going a bit haywire. I remember sitting down in a pub with Banny, Carl, Geoff and Jeanette and getting Pete over and saying, 'Er, we think your drug use is getting a bit out of control,' and he said, 'Yeah, I think you might be right,' so we were very

* Libertines' fan Morrissey later invited them to play at the 2004 Meltdown Festival he curated at London's Royal Festival Hall – a commitment they couldn't fulfil due to Pete's estrangement.

open about it, had a good chat about it and asked him to calm it down a bit."

You can't stop an individual following a path they choose for themselves, but I do sometimes wish I'd been better informed back then. What I know now is that there is no happy ending where crack cocaine is concerned. It's a destroyer. It's not something you dabble in – it'll consume you. And that's what it did to Pete Doherty.

CHAPTER 5

Livin' Rough, Looking Strange!

PETE was talking in reverential tones about a mysterious character called Wolfman. One drab Monday afternoon in early 2002,
we went to the lupine one's Clerkenwell dive and I was surprised
when the door opened and I realised who this Wolfman character
was. I'd actually known Pete Wolf since around 1999 when he used
to prop up the bar in a Primrose Hill pub, hounding Primal Scream
when they'd come in for a quiet jar. He was desperate for an inroad
into the music business, and on learning my flatmate Tara had
enjoyed moderate success in the early Nineties with a band called
5.30, he bombarded us with phone calls trying to forge a friendship.
A couple of years later he did likewise with another mate of mine,
Pete Voss, of Campag Velocet.

We regarded 'Wolfie' as a figure of fun, a bit of a buffoon – he
was calling himself 'Pete Nice', for fuck's sake. A friend of mine,
Mick, christened him 'Damon Hill-on-skag' as he resembled the
Formula One driver should a massive heroin habit befall him. It was
two, maybe three years since I'd last seen him and he'd clearly
descended into a smack hell quicker than Damon round a
Silverstone chicane. He eyed me with a mixture of suspicion and
astonishment when Pete D. introduced us.

This 'Wolfman' had clearly found the inroad into the music biz he so craved as Pete was obviously in thrall to him, elevating him to a kind of "smack sage" status. I knew better and thought this pairing could only end one way. Pretty soon, Wolfman was getting a bad press from the people at Rough Trade who were keen to distance Pete from anyone they believed to be a "bad influence". To me, Wolfman was just another in a long line of people playing Nancy to Pete's Sid. I don't mean to undermine his and Pete's friendship as they remain great mates. By the time he came to support The Libertines at the Forum in December 2003, he'd cultivated a pretty impressive stage act. Backed up by Britpop also-rans Rialto, his opening number was a John Cooper Clarke-style diatribe over a stinging repetitive guitar hook while 'For Lovers' was a gem of a tune which Pete would hijack a few months later and steer to number seven in the charts.

When he and Kill City later supported the Libs at Brixton Academy in March 2004, I was taken aback when, at the sound-check, a wasted Wolfie wrapped me in a tender embrace. Surveying the empty arena before us, he whispered in my ear, "Come a long way since Primrose Hill, ain't we Pete?" I got a contact high from his breath alone and while shocked at this sudden display of sickly sentimentality, I was genuinely touched. Squeezing his bony shoulder, I replied, "Not half, Pete."

Normal service was resumed a week later when he tried to eject me from Pete Doherty's flat in Whitechapel. I gave him the option: he could leave over the balcony or down the stairs while he had the chance. I've not seen him since. A shame really as Wolfman obviously has something to offer but is completely sold on the whole myth of rock'n'roll as self-destruction.

In February 2003, Pete invited me to accompany him to the lavish *NME* Awards where The Clash would be accepting a Godlike Genius award. Once again, he was considerate in knowing what it would mean to me to be there. We'd been up all the previous night and got to Hammersmith at about four in the afternoon, absolutely plastered, bumbling up the red carpet in shades and guards' jackets. The military jacket I'd borrowed off Pete to ensure a smooth entry was a beautiful Russian tank commander's jacket with epaulettes, badges – the works. "That's a bit dapper, ain't it Pete?" was Mick Jones' comment when I stumbled upon him. The jacket attracted so many compliments that I simply had to own it and a week later I traded Pete a Clash chord book for it.

The organisers were still laying the tables when we arrived. We caught the host, Bill Bailey, going through his lines, letting slip that The Libertines had scooped the Best Newcomer award. I was chuffed for Pete but he was relatively nonplussed and chose to sneak off to the loo for a pipe. With about 200 security men in the building I thought he was fucking mad but Pete was fearless, ominously gravitating toward danger like a moth to a flame, clearly believing he was a law unto himself.

As momentous as the evening was, with hindsight I can trace the demise of The Libertines back to that night. Pete had already been trying the others' patience with his unpredictable behaviour and earlier that afternoon, outside John Henry's equipment warehouse in Camden, I witnessed for the first time a snarling match between him and Carl. Exasperated by his partner's zombie-like demeanour, Carl tried to get Pete in range for a right-hander. Pete flinched as a clearly frustrated Carl, all pent-up like a coiled spring, motioned to chin him. I realised then that despite his height advantage, Pete clearly didn't fancy going toe-to-toe with his bandmate and I can't say I blamed him. A play fight in a Cardiff hotel room taught me that Carl Barat is a tough little fucker.

That night, when the band took to the stage to collect their award, Pete threw firecrackers with scant regard for anyone around him. Carl looked embarrassed. People thought it was crazy rock'n' roll behaviour but I could sense a gulf developing. The following week's *NME* featured a joke photo sequence of Pete at the ceremony in varying stages of disrepair, once again serving to galvanise his fledgling reputation as a Wildman. To those in the know, it was the first tangible sign of the car-crash-in-progress.

CARL: "We'd just got in there and we got called up onstage first, and as we're climbing up onto the stage I felt very emotional but it was like one of those moments in a comedy where the music is really glorious then it grinds to a halt, because Pete said, 'What the *fuck* are you wearing?' and I realised then that I had put my leather jacket over a suit jacket in the rush and I was embarrassed and disappointed and it kind of blew it for me really. It kind of felt right that we should win it though, without wanting to sound too self-righteous. Yeah it was a good feeling, and also because The Strokes had it the year before."

PETE: "I grew up reading the *NME* from a certain age but to be honest I didn't really give a fuck and I didn't really want to go. The truth is the girl who Carl had got off with the night before had taken a shine to me and that was that really. We had a little boogie and a few drinks and it had been a hell of a few days, all Subbuteo and crack-pipes up at The Albion Rooms, and the thought of a Scandinavian tour was heating the blood up already so I was all out for a bit of a giggle."

JAMES ENDEACOTT: "At the *NME* awards Pete was a little the worse for wear and it was a bit of a shame to see him up there not being himself. I wanted him to go up there and just be Pete and be funny and witty, but he was a little bit out of his mind that day which was sad to see really. He and Carl were always arguing but I never for once thought it was serious. They were always falling out and getting back together. It wasn't just the drugs, Carl was becoming mates with Danny [Goffey] from Supergrass and Pete was more involved with Pete Wolf and a little gulf was maybe developing. Carl was going down one route and Pete was going down another route, and both routes are valid, but they were different. Carl was spending less and less time at The Albion Rooms, which was becoming a place where kids just hung out. There was no water – you had to pour Evian down the loo to flush it. It was funny but it just didn't seem right. I mean I'm not a prude but you want some sense of normality."

GEOFF TRAVIS: "We've never really dealt with people on this level of drugs before – that we knew about. A lot of this has been brand new to us. It's been quite an emotional rollercoaster. Banny was pretty new to being a manager, she's a very bright girl and definitely had their best interests at heart, but was having a hard time dealing with them. That *NME* awards was a horrible night for me, I was really upset because I could see Peter was completely out of it. I hated every second of it and just went home. He wasn't the same person that we met. Getting an award just seemed ironic. They are a remarkable band and it's impossible not to love them but at the same time you have this horrible, empty feeling that it's all for nothing."

Around this time, I attended the launch of a short-lived music magazine, *Bang*, at Brick Lane's 93 Feet East club, where Pete was DJ-ing with The Queens of Noize. Further proof that the fellow was having some kind of identity crisis came when I saw him in the DJ booth dressed head-to-toe in full drag. Admittedly, he didn't look half-bad as a leggy blonde and sandwiched between Tabitha and Mairead, it was hard to tell who was who. It was good-natured fun but a bit daft all the same. Having said that, The Darkness were there to do a set – just before they went mega-huge – and in his spangly catsuit, their singer Justin Hawkins ran Pete close for the title of silliest fucker.

PETE: "There was definitely a tension on the bus going to do that Scandinavian tour but it was hidden away. Then as the tour routine developed, we'd both sleep whenever we were on the bus, wake up, stumble out and be forced into an interview, then be forced onstage. We'd be crash landing in places, getting absolutely obliterated again, forging a kind of bond onstage, going out somewhere and finding girls, then going different ways. Sleeping, waking up and doing it all over again. It was quite hard in Sweden to find drugs but the Pigman found the source! We met a right old punk who took me and Carl under his wings and took us to the sleaziest club, a proper rock'n'roll dive with all these garage kids. I remember fucking this girl in the toilets, on the floor, proper sort of sliding about the tiles and Carl came in with another girl, just as cool as you like and bent her over the disabled toilet. So there *were* those intimate, tender, romantic moments. Yeah, he had a smile on his face. And a vertical smile on his bum."

CARL: "It was quite surreal and beautiful, looking out the window over the fjords and what-have-you. There were still many feelings of togetherness. Shagging girls in toilets? Possibly. I dunno. You forget in Sweden, don't you?"

PETE: "On a slightly less dingy note we went somewhere, I can't remember where, but you had to fly there, then fly again, then get a coach. It was the most picturesque town and me and Carl got off the bus and went exploring together – walking up these really steep, cobbled streets, and old villages overlooking huge lakes, vast forests – really isolated. Anyway, we did the gig and afterwards I went up to the DJ and he wouldn't play The Smiths, or The Clash, so me and Carl tied him up in the DJ booth and started beating him up, actually. The bouncers came, these huge Vikings and literally beat us up and turfed us out.

"I remember in Switzerland we ended up in a state-sanctioned brothel, and it was a Rolling Stones-themed brothel, they'd only play the Stones and there was this big fat mama who ended up chasing us out. I remember Carl, he picked up a couple of brasses and he gave me the one he didn't really want, but I ended up being sick on her tits in the hotel room so she ran off. I had to listen all night to his bed squeaking. It was just girls, girls, girls. In Munich, I went off on a tandem with this girl, back to her place. She insisted on playing Suede. So it's afterwards and I want to go back to the venue because there's this other girl and I wanna get to her before Carl does, but the tandem-girl locks me in the bathroom so I think, 'Disaster,' and actually end up booting the door through and she was *screaming, screaming, screaming* and she was naked as well. She's had my clothes away, and I've had to jump back on her bike and race through the streets of Munich with just a hat on, back to the bus. And at the end of the night we had to leave Munich because we couldn't stay and Carl was just snogging this girl endlessly and I'm stood there like fucking Hancock, when Sid James has pulled and he hasn't. That was the girl that I'd cycled back for."

I didn't see too much of Pete over the next couple of months due to the band's touring commitments. From the outside it appeared fine and dandy but I was hearing reports to the contrary. The tension that I had witnessed at the *NME* awards bash seemed to intensify. Every time I'd see John or Gary they certainly didn't look like they were in the UK's best new band. They appeared tired and unhappy.

It should have been so different. The release in February of 'Time For Heroes' took them to number 15 in the charts and a memorable debut appearance on *Top Of The Pops*. Available in a two CD release format, the cover of one had Rabbi John, the bands' old mate from Filthy McNasty's. With characteristic irreverence they'd even let the old soak take the mic for one of the bonus tracks, the old standard 'Sally Brown' which would become a live staple.

PETE: "At *Top Of The Pops* you make your own amusement, running around the corridors. Carlos, of course, was lording it up a bit as he once worked as the photocopier boy or whatever at the BBC and he was treated like a nothing, like a dogsbody, and now he was back swinging his axe about. Mick Jones came down and it was drinks all round. We met The Cheeky Girls' mum. Busted were there too."

CARL: "Yeah, I did used to work there. I went into my old office to have a good gloat at the woman who sacked me but of course the office was closed so it was a bit of a hollow victory. Pete wasn't looking well, he said, 'Come on, let's go to make-up,' and I thought, 'OK, I could do with a bit of touching up myself.' I went in there and he was really excited, bless him, but he looked like a lady-boy. He'd made his hair enormous like some sort of New Romantic thing, his face was pale white and he had big red lipstick on. He looked atrocious. I wouldn't let him go through with it – for *his* sake. He just didn't look well, he didn't look appealing and he didn't look like anything that had previously been to do with The Libertines. He started crying, he was really upset and I felt really bad but I just couldn't have gone on.

"Cheeky Girls, they were a bunch, and Girls Aloud were there too which pleased me no end. I went up to their dressing room and I was all jolly, and slightly merry, and I opened the door and said, rather crassly, 'Are there any boys allowed?' and was met with a lot of blank expressions. Even the ones that are slightly rough, they sort of fit into the fray and they all become fit, that's the appeal of those girls, isn't it? Even the Spice Girls all looked fit at one point.

"The audience are utterly enamoured to be there, awe-struck, so they're delighted to clap for anything. It was very strange to see a bunch of people who we knew had never heard of us applauding us so boisterously. It was very confusing and kind of indicative of what was to come really, in terms of the tabloid attention."

'Time For Heroes' saw The Libertines shaping up to be one of the great British singles bands. Premature comparisons were drawn with The Kinks but, to my mind, the band followed an uncannily similar trajectory to The Buzzcocks. For 'Orgasm Addict' read 'What A Waster' — a debut single of deliciously dubious content, instantly outlawed by the industry. With 'Up The Bracket', 'Time For Heroes' and later, 'Don't Look Back Into The Sun', The Libertines adopted the same unpretentious punk-pop sensibility that had sequenced 'What Do I Get?', 'Ever Fallen In Love' and 'Promises' 25 years earlier.

TONY LINKIN: "They weren't *brilliant* early on, they really weren't. James Oldham wrote that fantastic review in the *NME* saying they were like The Beatles at the Cavern and stuff — they definitely *could* do that but they were very hit and miss at that point, they just hadn't done enough gigs really. But that UK tour, early in 2003, they actually did really well. I saw them in Nottingham and they were everything I ever wanted them to be, they were really off on it, becoming the best band in the country. Unfortunately that was the last gig, and then there was the Germany thing where Pete didn't make it.

"Pete really changed a lot from the chubby lad we all met at the beginning. He was looking more like a rock star, very charismatic. Part of it was the drugs, part of it was natural. It was a combination. I think when they first met, Carl had always had the upper hand over Pete being a year older, and then I think Pete gradually was the worm that turned, as he said in one interview."

ROGER SARGENT: "We were coming back from Nottingham, a gig at The Rescue Rooms, and a few people were getting dropped off. Then they were carrying straight on to Germany. I remember all the way back Pete was quite agitated, and you kind of got the impression that he'd had a really good time but he didn't want to go any further. The Nottingham show had been fucking mental. I just remember he kept asking me on the bus, 'Where are we stopping in London?' and 'Maybe I could just nip off?'"

JAMES ENDEACOTT: "They were meeting in King's Cross to go to Germany and Pete wanted to go and see somebody. He and Banny had a row and he ended up just running off the bus, and they left without him. They had to tour – they'd have been sued, absolutely sued to the hilt. Carl taught the guitar tech Pete's parts."

PETE: "There was a weird atmosphere on the bus. I was saying to Banny how things were OK but she said, 'Well they're not OK, Pete, *everybody's* complaining about your behaviour, you're out of control, you've got no respect, etc, etc.' I said, 'Banny, you're wrong, everyone's fine,' and she said, 'No, that's just what they say to you, but they complain to me.' [That day the band's third tour manager – who had worked with some of the industry's biggest and most "difficult" artists, had called Banny threatening to quit, claiming Peter had totally undermined him and his ability to do his job. The band's chief roadie was also alarmed at the increasing violence of the stage invasions which forced him to act as a human shield, preventing the drum kit from collapsing on Gary and causing serious damage. He claimed he had tried to speak to Peter but it was falling on deaf ears.] Boom, boom, boom, sinister music started in my brain and I couldn't deal with that. So I nipped off at King's Cross to score. I just wanted Carl to put his arm around my shoulder and come for a walk with me. So they said I was ill – bronchial pneumonia. The thing was I did actually have bronchial pneumonia but it had never stopped me before. I've still got it. I think if we'd done that tour things would probably be OK today."

CARL: "Pete got off the bus at King's Cross and never got back on. He wanted me to go with him 'on an adventure' but I knew what that really meant was to go and get some crack, and so he had the hump with me for not going with him. I wasn't really into following him at that time. The bus went on and there was talk of him flying out to Hamburg but by the time we got to Hamburg it was bitterly cold and I was a bit toured-out, and *I* had pneumonia; only mild, like, but enough to make me not want to do the gig, to brazen it out on my own. He never made it out: he was sat in Banny's flat, apparently tearful and just messed-up in general. [Pete failed to fly out to Hamburg with Banny and Carl was too ill to tour alone. The band returned to England and cancelled the March European tour. When Pete failed to show for the second European tour in June 2003, the band chose to press on without him.]

"We continued to tour, in good faith to Pete, but as in any hiatus, I kept my ear to the ground and through the grapevine what I heard was Pete wasn't making any progress or recovery, or self-realisation about the *danger* of his plight, and I was forced to carry on touring alone. It then became one of those silly power situations where Pete said he might, if he fancied it, join us in Spain, but of course he never made it.

"We got as far as Paris and through the grapevine and from keeping a close eye on what was happening in England I learnt Pete's situation had worsened to such an intensity that he was a danger not only to himself but to all those around him. This broke my heart to see 'cos I'm talking about a *friend* here, and so the hardest phone call of my life came when I got to Paris when I had to be the one to say, 'I don't think you should come to Paris to do the show tonight,' and that phone call is something I'll never forget for the rest of my life."

PETE: "I didn't really want to go on that tour too much. I wanted to stay in London. I *had* to stay in London in a way. But they ran off without me, and then my Aunt Lil died so I stayed in London for the funeral, by which time they had obviously built up the strength within themselves, and built up a vibe with the new fella and thought, 'Well, we don't actually *need* him, who's he to swan in and out when he feels like it?' and then I said to Banny, 'Look, I'm coming whether you like it or not,' and she said, 'Well, no, because Carl actually doesn't want you.' I said, 'No, that's not true, you can't speak for Carl, Carl would *never, ever* turn me away from a gig, whatever state I was in, he would always let me in,' and she said, 'Well, ask him yourself.' When I phoned him he was on the ferry coming over to do the Manchester and London shows, and he said it. He actually said it, but it *wasn't him*. Well, it *was* him but it didn't sound like him, it sounded so distant and so fucked-up. It took me half-an-hour really, to thaw him out a bit, to get a voice that I recognised as the Carl that I knew and loved.

"All the time he was saying that I had become a person that he didn't know, but I was faced with this person that *I really didn't know*. When I first met Carl he was a heavy drug user and I wasn't. I saw through that and I believed in him. But with him the problem was the people I was with and the environments I was in, but then again Carl wouldn't have even known; all he was getting was second- and third-hand reports."

The spring of 2003 saw The Libertines play a series of smaller venues like The Buffalo Bar and The Monarch and it was during these shows that they really cemented their reputation as "band of the people", displaying an accessibility and willingness to press flesh with their growing legion of fans. Kill City supported a couple of times and this was the first time I really got the impression that this band had the potential to go stellar. Everyone wanted a piece of them. Gordon Raphael, the near-legendary producer of both Strokes albums and London resident, could be spotted at most shows, unashamedly proclaiming his desire to get behind the desk to produce their next sessions. "It's like meeting The Beatles when they were 18 years old," he gushed. These smaller gigs would soon give way to the infamous guerrilla gigs that Pete pioneered at The Albion Rooms. While these shows were unprecedented (imagine Oasis playing in your local or your mate's flat?), they would soon become a bone of contention between the two brothers-in-arms, and a divisive force that would ultimately contribute to the band's monumental crash, and spawn the (first) coming of Babyshambles.

ROGER SARGENT: "I got a phone call from Carl saying, 'You've got to come along, we're doing a farewell to The Albion Rooms,' because I think at that stage he'd kind of had enough of all the partying, and the coming-and-going. It was still sort of jolly but I think he just needed to get out. They put it on the web that they were having a little shindig there, charging people a nominal fee and it would be free drinks; I think there were about 10 cans of lager. The thing is, no one had done anything like that before and consequently when something like that got advertised on the net, no one was gonna *believe* it. Then after the first couple of times, people were like, 'Bloody hell, this is really going to happen.'"

PETE: "There wasn't any enthusiasm from Carl, or John and Gary for those gigs, those smaller gigs. I think the praise and the interest that came from it, they were happy to receive but there wasn't the basic desire to just do it, which *I had*, the pleasure and excitement of doing it. It was wicked, still is. I just realised, hang on a minute, 'We can do it, we can do these sorts of things.'"

CARL: "I loved doing the gigs, I just didn't want to charge — I wanted to do the gigs for free. You know, the kids who are gonna hike across town at the last minute and pay a tenner are the same kids who are gonna hike across town at the last minute and come in for free so it wasn't like we were at the risk of no one coming. I remember seeing on the internet kids saying they couldn't afford it but that they were gonna beg, borrow or steal to get the money. So I thought, 'Well, what am I gonna do with the money? I probably won't see any of it anyway because there's always some kind of shenanigans involved when it comes to sharing out the proceeds?' and it just left a bit of a bad taste in my mouth around that time."

TONY LINKIN: "I didn't like going round to the house at that point. The people that Pete started having around, Carl didn't like it really. When they first lived together it was fantastic, they really worked. They'd sit there all night writing together, singing together. It was such a fantastic place to go round. But it all went a bit sour towards the end. Pete got locked out one night and knocked the door down, the lock came off and then someone just walked in the door and nicked all Carl's stuff."

CARL: "I wanted my own space. I had a flimsy room with a partition wall and a broken door. There was just no privacy, Pete knows this: I've always needed *some* privacy, maybe it comes from travelling a lot as a kid. That's what eventually led to me leaving; when the Pete-posse are in town, doing what they're doing, there's no escape and when I wasn't there they were all in my little bit anyway, piping on my bed and stuff. Things were going missing and getting turned upside down. I had to leave that place."

With the chaotic goings-on at home and the turbulence and uncertainty of their recent European sojourn, the timing of The Libertines' inaugural US tour was hardly ideal. The band were on a knife-edge, and their headline set at the Coachella Festival in California saw the plug being pulled two songs in. It didn't bode well, and set the tone for a stormy few weeks.

TONY LINKIN: "They went off to America with Pete, but that turned sour. They tried recording out there and Pete brought some crack guy into the studio that he'd just met, who also joined them onstage. Pete was off all night so people were worried about whether he'd turn up."

ROGER SARGENT: "I got out to New York and met up with them outside CBGBs and my whole thing was, 'Wow, I'm in New York with The Libertines, I've *got* to document this,' but I couldn't get them all in the same place for more than five minutes. I thought we should do a photo-shoot by way of a tour of New York, but I literally *could not* keep them together. I think someone had told Pete that if you ever want to score in the States, or whatever, then just go up to a homeless person and they'll tell you where to get it and he'd really taken this on board. So we were outside CBGBs in the Bowery, which is not the nicest area, and they've done the soundcheck, and I just see Pete wandering down the street and going up to homeless bloke after homeless bloke. I think that's how he met the crack dealer guy who joined them onstage. He managed to convince Pete that he had some kind of musical background – the fucker couldn't sing! Jesus, it was actually quite excruciating."

CARL: "It was always my dream to get to America but never to go as a tourist, always to go when I was involved in something. I always thought it would be to do films but as it turned out it was with this, but I was equally proud. There were so many *good* times. When you're living in a bad instant, the history of the world seems bad, whereas when you get the little stabs at happiness that is also all-encompassing. It wasn't just the drugs and the impact they had on Pete's personality and our relationship, but it was the people that surrounded him. He came up to my room, Endeacott was there, all wide-eyed and tearful saying, 'I can't handle it any more,' and sending me down to kick some crack heads out of his room, which isn't easy when they're there for the free drugs. I didn't want to do it but I found myself biting bullets for my friend – he wanted my display of doing that more than he wanted them out of his room by all accounts."

JAMES ENDEACOTT: "It was weird because we had to cancel the first night in San Francisco because Pete's grandmother died, and we eventually met him at the airport in LA and there was a bit of a mood of 'What's it going to be like?' but we got there and it was great. It was really great to see him, and him and Carl had such a great time at the Coachella Festival, nicking these little golf buggies, hanging out with Primal Scream who had a van next to ours. It all started to go wrong when we spent the last 10 days of the trip in New York and we were staying in a hotel called Off Soho Suites. Pete found a crack dealer within two hours of getting to New York and just started hanging out with him all the time. There were three shows in New York and Pete turned up literally five minutes before each gig, nobody knew where he was. They were three mind-blowing gigs, but then he left five minutes afterwards – we just didn't see Pete.

"It was a very tense time but they played some really great gigs on that American tour, a really great gig in Seattle, but the tension really happened in New York. We all left and Pete smashed up his hotel room at The Chelsea Hotel, and tried to smash up our offices out there. He was just out of his mind and it was a really horrible time. There were a *lot* of drugs going down, I remember at the Bowery Ballroom, Pete dragged on this crack dealer to do a song."

PETE: "Within five hours of being in New York I had a homeless crack bum living in my hotel room, washing-up, these twins, a couple of Sixties freaks, and the daughter of a politician all in my bed. There was the point when we went out to Philadelphia and I sat at the back of the minibus blowing fumes of crack into the back of Gary's head. You could have cut the atmosphere with a fucking cake knife. Banny, James Endeacott, Gary and John up front, Carl, doing line after line after line, sat next to me. I remember singing 'Horrorshow' a cappella just to remind them all who's boss.

"CBGBs was probably the most out-of-tune, discordant, uncomfortable half an hour of Libertines music by a long way. Carl and I were both in despair, we were in America and there was no effort being made by anyone. No one was reaching out to us, no one was communicating with us – neither audience nor record company. I went round there and asked if I could use the internet and they literally didn't trust me to be in the office, just using the internet. They wouldn't trust me so they made all kinds of excuses. I lost it. I told them they hadn't had the news yet, but I'd become a millionaire and bought Rough Trade so I actually owned the office, and they couldn't stop me. They tried to remove me, and I ended up pushing the computer off the desk, and smashing a bottle of red wine against the wall. Some giffer in a pair of long shorts, he thought the music industry involved a fax machine and a promotional CD – he had no concept of human beings. I *needed* to use the internet. I didn't want to fucking lay on the floor and inject anything into my eyeball.

"I was just a lost fucking soul, completely alone, completely cut off by Carl. I couldn't put up with the heartache of being completely exiled, not being taken seriously or shown any respect by the band, the management, the record company, the accountant. I was treated like a monster, or a child. The gigs were my only escape. Most people involved with The Libertines, as fans, or on a professional level, probably a few of the first words they *ever* would have heard me say would be, 'I'm a swine and you don't wanna know me,' [*from 'Horrorshow'*], OK? So I've laid my cards down on the table from the start. I've explained the problem, I've explained the way it is, but that also suggests someone who's willing to try and understand things, and *learn*. So if you're gonna get involved, *don't* dip your toe in the water, dive in and immerse yourself, right? I *can* be a swine, but I'm not really, and I'm not a violent, socially corrupt person. I'm gentle and try to be positive with myself. But the more people who mistrust me or disrespect me, the more likely I am to play them up."

CARL: "After I'd left, after I'd had to fly back to England because I had family problems, [Pete] ended up having some delusional tantrum where I think he uttered the words, 'I own Rough Trade, I own Sanctuary,' when they asked him to leave the office – some kind of peculiar megalomania at play there?"

JAMES ENDEACOTT: "Going to the airport with John and Gary, John had a real go at me saying, 'You've got to fucking sort him out.' John saw me as part of the problem I think, because I was doing drugs with him, though not the heavy drugs.

"*The David Letterman Show* is in The Ed Sullivan Theatre on 53rd Street, just up from Times Square, a really tall old building. We were on the top floor in this tiny little dressing room, and Marilyn Manson had his next to us. All of a sudden over the tannoy it says, 'Can Marilyn Manson please come to the stage,' and he walks past the dressing room with these big bouncers, and Pete and Carl shout, 'Oi Brian, Brian!' because he's called Brian, and they ran out after him to the elevator. I followed, but the elevator shut in front of them. Quick as a flash, they just ran down the stairs to the next floor and pressed the button, so when he got to the next floor the door opened and Manson's confronted by Pete and Carl with an acoustic guitar going, 'We'll meet again, don't know when, don't know where, etc, etc.' and Manson goes [*adopts deep American accent*], 'Funny guys, funny guys.'"

PETE: "Outside *Letterman*, I remember having a hat on and a pair of sunglasses that I'd found and pretending to be Marilyn Manson's brother. I just happened to fall out of a car with blacked-out windows and there was hordes of kids down there going, 'Are you with Marilyn Manson?' because I had a guitar, and I go [adopts American stoner-accent], 'Yeah, I'm playing guitar with him today, I'm actually his stepbrother, man,' and, 'Man, I'm buzzed out,' and there was *a furore.*

"I remember it being Carl's day. I think Carl was the star in America, we even talked about going to South America and calling ourselves *Carlos and Los Libertines*, no seriously, we were gonna do it. On *Letterman* we did 'I Get Along' and even though he didn't write it, it's still seen as Carl's song, and I don't sing on it at all of course. I was fucking glad to be doing it, but for all Carl's talk of us being together and there being no frontman, he didn't seem to understand what it meant to me. I thought for us to do a song that we both sung on might have brought us together. The fella from *Jackass* was there and he was buzzing, going, 'That was fucking great, man.'"

JAMES ENDEACOTT: "Everybody was in high spirits but after we'd done the soundcheck, there was nothing to do for four hours, so everyone started going off on their own separate ways. I was really worried about where Pete was going to go so I waited outside and as he came out, I said, 'Where you going Pete, I've got nothing to do for hours?' and he says he's going to St. Mark's Place to buy some clothes. I felt bad because I was doing it so I could keep my eye on him, but we were in a yellow New York cab, it was a hot day and I remember the conversation really well. Pete said, 'James, we're just about to do David Letterman, I'm in New York, I can't believe how I've got here.' I said, 'Pete, *I* can't believe how we've got here,' and he said, 'Mate, this is one of the greatest days of my life, this is fucking amazing.' We went for clothes, and then for cocktails, and then back and did it. They did 'I Get Along' and they were all in the red jackets and I just thought, 'It's The Libertines *on David Letterman*, it's going out to millions and millions of people,' and they were so tight. The interesting thing about *Letterman* is it was the last time

Pete played with The Libertines until the night he came out of prison in Chatham – that was the madness."

CARL: "Another pie-in-the-sky idea I'd had in my acting days was that one day I'd play to a theatre on Broadway, and the day I *did* play to a full house on Broadway, I played to 60 million people across the country, which is a fair few. We did 'I Get Along'. I don't know whether Pete wanted to do a song we both sang on or one that just he sang on, but I don't like having to watch my back all the time, for this competition really, it does my head in. Because I don't like being usurped, I feel I have to be competitive, but I don't like having to do that."

ROGER SARGENT: "It was compounded by the fact you couldn't smoke in any of the bars, and I really do blame this for a lot of the things about that trip. They just weren't hanging out. I remember going into Pete's room with Carl, and Pete offering me a pipe and I said, 'Nah, no thanks Pete.' I mean apart from anything else Carl would have gone apeshit. They tried to do some recording and it was horrible, really horrible. We kind of joke about it now but it was one of the most upsetting times I've had with them. It really was."

PETE: "I remember being enticed into some scary situations, in tenement projects, with blaring fucking dark beats with all kinds of things going on around me. The fellas I was meeting on the street and just getting involved with. Miss Dynamite, not the one you know, but this white girl in New York, she basically raped me to the tune of 'Is she worth it?' [*'In Da Club' by 50 Cent*]. At one point I had her fucking straddling me, another fella lighting a pipe, and another fella cutting my hair, black fellas. Nuts."

CHAPTER 6

Road To Ruin

AT the end of May, shortly after he'd returned from the eventful American tour, Pete called and invited me over to Wolfman's new abode in Gunter Grove, at the Fulham end of King's Road. It was hard to believe that rock's most rising star was technically homeless and staying on various mates' couches for a few nights at a time. I arrived in the early afternoon where I found Pete on his own in this hole of a basement, wearing shabby shell suit bottoms. He struck me as decidedly forlorn. However, this was very much the calm before the storm as a secret Libertines gig had been arranged for later that night in this very place.

They've since become known as "guerrilla gigs", or "Spontaneous Arcadian Knees-ups" as Pete prefers – his idea of organising a show over the internet at short notice. Newer bands like The Others have taken the form to the extreme with shindigs on tube trains and up trees – in a way an extension of the "flashmob" craze – but to Pete it was a quick and easy way of putting a show together. You could organise a gig in the morning, circulate the location on the busy fan forum at lunchtime, and by that evening, you'd have a paying audience on the doorstep. Whether this new concept was Pete's altruistic way of "keeping it real" or a cynical money-making ruse or even both, I don't know, but the kids certainly didn't begrudge the eight quid entrance charge.

Gary turned up later that afternoon as Pete and I were getting the gaff ready. He took one look at the druggy crowd that was starting to assemble and left, not to be seen again. John was not involved anyway, but Carl was pencilled in to appear alongside Pete. He didn't turn up either – a move that was to have further repercussions.

By about nine o'clock there were 100 or so fans crammed into the basement flat with Pete entertaining them with his acoustic in the garden, kitchen, front room – almost everywhere. It was a real sweat box and a considerable fire hazard. Inevitably, the boys in blue were soon on the scene in force. It was left to me to head off the old bill and try to prevent them from making arrests and busting the main organisers. Pete characteristically didn't give a shit and carried on playing. It was comical really. 'What A Waster' became a mass sing-a-long with the hapless plod trying to break it up. It put me in mind of The Beatles' rooftop show on the Apple building.

One guy's helmet came off as a bit of jostling ensued but for the most part, they were reasonable and by 10 o'clock it was all over, with everyone spilling out into the front garden and onto the street. The fun wasn't over just yet as the inhabitant of the upstairs flat, a burly bloke who didn't dig the racket, put the window through and gave Wolfman a smack in the mouth for good measure.

While the kids were content enough with a solo Pete, I sensed that he was quite hurt that Carl had voted with his feet. The gaping chasm between the two friends was widening even more.

PETE: "I really needed Carl to show that night, really needed him to show and he didn't, and then it appeared in the *NME* in a news article. I remember Carl phoning me up and saying, 'You *bastard*,' in a kind of jokey way, basically saying, 'Why didn't you get *me* down

Carl backstage at the Marquee before the Xfm Christmas party with The Darkness, December 2002. *(Pete Welsh Collection)*

The band on stage at the Xfm Christmas party.
(Pete Welsh Collection)

Carl with Danny Goffey from Supergrass,
Christmas 2002. *(Pete Welsh Collection)*

The author and Pete toast the New Year in Camden,
2002, not knowing how tumultuous it would be.
(Pete Welsh Collection)

Pole-dancing in Basel, Switzerland, 2003.
(Pete Welsh Collection)

With James Endeacott at *Top Of The Pops*
for 'Time for Heroes', 24 January, 2003.
(Pete Welsh Collection)

John en route to the stage, Nottingham. February 2003.
(Pete Welsh Collection)

Backstage at the Lux, Brooklyn, May 2003.
(Roger Sargent)

The infamous Gunter Grove gig, Pete and Wolfman, May 2003.
(Pete Welsh Collection)

The Pied Piper: Pete treating some fans to a 'Libertine' tattoo, Soho, May 2003.
(Pete Welsh Collection)

The calm before the storm – Gunter Grove, May 2003.
(Pete Welsh Collection)

Thick as thieves just before the break-ins, Soho, July 2003.
(Pete Welsh Collection)

This was the photo that so shocked Carl. The author and Pete shortly before his arrest, July 2003. *(Pete Welsh Collection)*

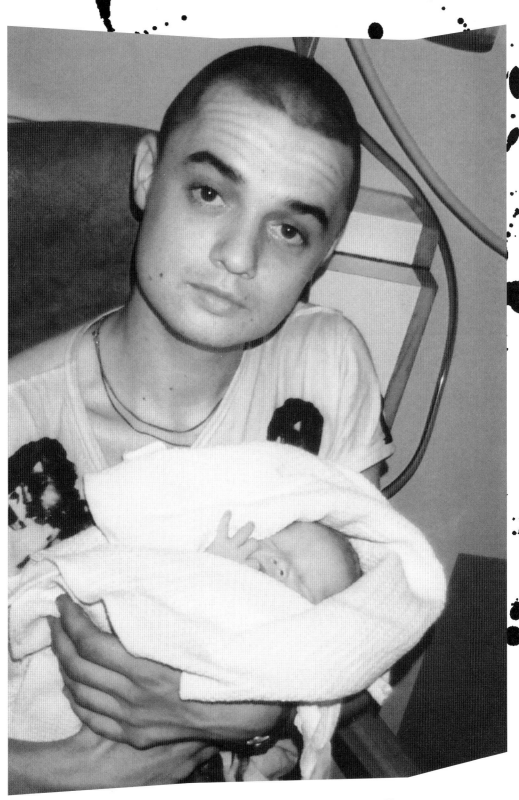

Pete with his and Lisa's new-born son Astile, July 2003.
(Pete Welsh Collection)

Meet the new boss – Pete with Alan McGee, October 2003.
(Pete Welsh Collection)

there?' and I said, 'You were invited, man. I was telling you about it constantly. Why didn't you come?' and he went, 'Yeah, but I didn't know it was going to be in the press.' It broke my heart really. I didn't know it was going to be in the press either. I didn't even want it to be in the press. It came as a shock that they would even want to report it; it was a fucking *party in a flat* that turned into a bit of an acoustic gig, and then they reported it with more fucking coverage than they'd ever reported a proper gig!

"So we met up in Regent's Park, a fateful day, and we had a long chat about everything. He said it was his birthday coming up and he might be busy that one particular night, so I explained I was gonna do another gig on this rooftop in Whitechapel and would he come and play? He said he'd love to, and I said, 'If you say you're gonna come, come, because people are gonna come from Scotland probably, and Wales and God-knows-where, so you're gonna have to come if you say.' And he didn't. And he didn't *phone*. And that was that. *That was that.* I was a bit *deranged* really. It just didn't compute that this one person, probably the *only* person who had all my love and trust would, like, knowingly break my fucking heart. And I know his heart was breaking for different reasons, but I *needed* him to be there."

CARL: "I guess it was a kind of 'getting-money-and-showing-off'-type do rather than wanting to give a gig. It upset me because it was on my birthday and I'd told him the day before that my sister had organised me something, and he was saying, 'Well finish it early and come and do this gig.' So I get there and enjoy my birthday for a bit with a few drinks, surrounded by friends and people who really cared about, you know, their friend, then I say, 'Sorry, I've got to leave, everyone, I've got to go and do this gig.' A lot of them looked at me in disgust, like, 'How ridiculous,' and a number of people barricaded the doorway, which I think was fair to be honest. I'd been hoodwinked into doing something that wasn't fair and that I didn't want to do and Pete should have shown more consideration."

The day after the Gunter Grove gig I met up with Pete in Soho at a Chinatown pub where he used to work behind the bar. It was a glorious summer's day and we enjoyed a few drinks to wind down from the long night before. Not wanting the party to end, Pete had invited the kids left over from the gig to join us and after more lubrication he decided to fritter the takings from the show on tattoos for all and sundry at a tattoo parlour by the Raymond Revue bar. I think he splashed out about 300 quid for his seven or eight young disciples to get ankles, forearms and feet inscribed with the legend "libertine". I decided to sit this one out, watching incredulously as these youngsters queued up to get inked. I couldn't help thinking there would be a few irate dads keen to get their hands on the pied piper.

I'd seen enough by this point and headed back to Kentish Town. I'd only been home an hour before the phone rang. It was Pete, ringing from The Good Mixer, out of his nut and spoiling for a scrap with an *NME* journalist who he believed to have dissed him. "Sit tight," I said, "I'm on my way, you fucking header." I got to the pub in about 10 minutes flat, to be met by Pete. "There he is, the cunt, let's do him!" I looked over to see an old pal of mine who had sod all to do with the *NME*, enjoying a quiet pint at the bar, oblivious to the imminent hiding Pete was supposedly going to inflict upon him. "Come on you daft bastard," I said as I helped him walk. "Let's get you home." Pete had other ideas, however. I left him hustling for bad shit with some of the less desirable occupants of Inverness Street, and walked home in disgust.

TONY LINKIN: "The reason Pete gave for not going to Germany was because Carl never came to that gig at Wolfman's house, but although it was Carl's birthday party that night, he fully intended to go. All his family were there though, making it difficult for him to leave. Personally I don't think that's enough of a reason not to go to Germany but there was probably a lot more going on under the surface."

JAMES ENDEACOTT: "That summer it was really messy. Pete sort of distanced himself from us, he did come around the office now and again wanting money, tapping up money and I could see him wasting away in front of me. I never went to all those early Pete shows, I kept away."

Those first guerrilla gigs over the summer of 2003 would often be in bizarre venues. I remember one in The Red Rose Labour club, on the Seven Sisters Road, a real old man's boozer, supported by Wolfman. Instead of a plush backstage area, Pete was outside the venue sat in the back of a tatty transit van, chugging away on a pipe. He was starting to go "off the map", to use the current vernacular, and his performance that night climaxed with a mass stage invasion, with Pete ad-libbing the names of obscure QPR footballers from the Eighties and Nineties into the mic to a messy backbeat. It went over the young Libertines fans' heads, who hadn't a clue who the likes of Roy Wegerle or Gary Bannister were, but such was the fervour for Pete by this stage, he could have farted into the mic and got a frenzied reaction.

The presence of *NME* journalists at the gigs had the demeanour of curious visitors to a freak show and I found it irresponsible of them to publish weekly bulletins on Babyshambles' progress, or lack of. Pete was by this stage feeding off his own twisted hype and they were giving him all the oxygen of publicity he needed. If they hadn't afforded him this, I believe he might have wrapped the whole sorry affair up a lot sooner than he did. While Carl and, to a much lesser degree, the other Libs were no saints, the whole scene surrounding Babyshambles was unashamedly sordid and negative, putting me in mind of Sid Vicious assembling a motley crew, the

Vicious White Kids to back him, ironically at the Electric Ballroom in Camden Town, exactly 25 years earlier. Vicious was dead within several months, and while I don't want to play up the analogy, everyone close to Pete had justifiable fears.

One early summer's evening, me, Pete and a gaggle of the usual suspects wound up back at Katie Bapples' Belsize Park flat. Later on Katie would be one of a number of two-bit hangers-on who'd sell their story to the tabloids; in her case she accused Pete of carving her up with a razor blade. Of course, love. Another kid, barely out of her teens, surfaced claiming to have been Pete's squeeze for the last couple of years. Well, if she was she must have been the stay-at-home type because I'd never clapped eyes on her.

Pete had this new song 'What Katie Did', a lovely ditty that later turned up on *The Libertines*. Somehow, in the middle of the night, we had access to a 4-track portastudio and set about recording it. It had a backing vocal refrain of "shoop, shoop, du-lang du-lang" with Pete and I playing guitars and the assembled kids just about managing to commit a passable rendition to tape. But when it came to an elementary handclap or finger-click in time with the beat it took two fucking hours and they were still no nearer to an acceptable take. Now I'm no virtuoso but I like to think I can whistle and walk at the same time. I slipped off home blinking in the light, walking and chewing gum simultaneously just to reassure myself I hadn't had my sense of rhythm sapped out of me by Pete's numbskull crew.

By June, Pete was officially out of The Libertines. That same month, I went to see the band at the Kentish Town Forum as a guest of Gary's. It was their first headlining show at a large venue and Pete Doherty wasn't there – a sad state of affairs. They put on a good show with Carl manfully handling frontman duties, if looking a little shell-shocked and resigned. Standing high up in the top tier, I could only manage a few numbers. It didn't feel right and I got a bit choked up.

Carl would later describe taking the stage without Pete as feeling "like a public execution, like waking up to the gallows." Although Pete's drug problem was an open secret, Barat's admission in the July 12 edition of *NME* that "some strong forces took [Pete] away" was the first indication from a published source as to the cause of his absence.

CARL: "I didn't enjoy it, it was quite a shock to the system really, but I did it for the good of the band, and for the good of keeping promises, and loyalty and having dignity in what you're doing. It was pretty horrible actually."

ROGER SARGENT: "The first time I'd seen them without Peter was at Glastonbury. It was just loads of people slapping Carl on the back going, 'You've pulled it off,' which I know he didn't really want people saying. That gig was really important to Carl, because Glastonbury's his thing, you know? He didn't want to be playing it without Peter. There were rumours all weekend that he was going to turn up. I think him being welcomed back would have been more feasible than if he'd turned up at Reading/Leeds. They'd got a new tour manager and a whole new crew around them specifically to deal with Peter, and then he wasn't there so it was kind of a false start. I think if he had turned up it would have been all right."

JAMES ENDEACOTT: "[Pete] was in a bad way, it just wasn't working. He was never thrown out of the band, he was just *so* unreliable and hopefully Pete realises this. They just couldn't do it. It was a really nasty time. The sessions for the new single were really fraught, he only lasted about a day and a half in the studio, him and Bernard [Butler] had a really big row and the band just carried on, and then the single came out and Pete wasn't involved in the artwork which was a real shame as he'd always done the artwork.

There was no video so we had to cobble one together. Then they did *Top Of The Pops* without him which I think was a really big mistake. Pete's relationship with Banny was also breaking down. Pete obviously didn't like the mechanics of the touring and the press. It got a bit too much for him."

TONY LINKIN: " 'Don't Look Back Into The Sun' was quite fraught because Pete's drug habits were getting worse. He would turn up really late and Carl just couldn't stand him being so out of it, I suppose. They were there to work really and Bernard, who's a lovely fella, didn't really want to suffer it whereas Mick [Jones] is a bit more prepared to take it as it comes. Bernard and Pete fell out. Bernard basically stood up to him in the studio. He would turn up wasted and Bernard would be like, 'Come back when you're not wasted.' The atmosphere was not great, they were all very depressed. They wanted Pete to be in the studio with them, recording."

GEOFF TRAVIS: "Pete was hardly there, he did his vocal and that was it. Bernard played his guitar parts."

CARL: "We wrote 'Don't Look Back Into The Sun' together in Paris. Recording it was very problematic and there were a lot of tears and a fair bit of silliness. I think Bernard actually dealt very well with it. I'd never ever seen Pete have a temper tantrum, ever, until the drugs came about. Not in that sporadic, irrational, out-of-nowhere sense. Pete spent very little time in there and we did most of it without him. His vocal was compiled on pro-tools. It took a while to get that together. It was quite a troublesome session really."

PETE: "I mustered the courage to take myself along to RAK Studios with the Wolfman as my spiritual guide. He pushed me out the door and I bowled on down the street alone and in a daze. I phoned Bernard Butler to say I'm coming. He said, 'You're running a bit late, aren't you? Don't bother coming at all.' I said, 'Bernard, I'm not doing a nine to five. I'm in the right frame of mind.' I walked into the studio to them playing 'Eight Days A Week'. Me and Carl greeted each other, it wasn't to do with the band, it wasn't to do with the record, and we arranged to meet later because we just presumed things were going to go a little bit awry in the next couple of hours and sure enough within an hour I'd threatened to knock Bernard out. He commented on my behaviour and my attitude and asked me to leave. It was his *tone* really, more than *what* he said."

ROGER SARGENT: "The thing about Bernard is he's quite a good taskmaster, but Peter doesn't take any form of authority very well. One time I went down there Pete had disappeared to meet his man; this is when he really started flaunting doing the pipe and stuff. For the other guys, by this stage, it had become more than just an irritant, but it hadn't got to the point where everybody thought it was *serious* serious. You have to bear in mind that the very first tour that I went on, before the 'Up The Bracket' tour even, there was a bit of foil going around and I said to Pete, 'You've really got to fucking watch that, I've seen so many people go the wrong way,' and he was like, 'Nah, don't worry, I'll never get addicted to it.' How *those* words have rung around in my head.

"They went in after 'Don't Look Back Into The Sun' to do 'Last Post On The Bugle' with Bernard, and at every opportunity, Pete would try to get the pipe out in front of Bernard and get me to do a photo of it. I think he actually asked him to leave the studio a couple of times. That was why, when they went in to do the second album, McGee brought in the twins to do security."

PETE: "It was when we did the session for 'Likely Lads' and 'Last Post' that John took me down the pub and we had a proper chat, the first time in a long time. We got on OK but it was intolerably fucking numbing to the senses because he wasn't really listening to *me.* I was listening to him but it was quite blinkered, his view of things."

One of the causes of Pete's protracted exile from The Libertines, aside from his obvious narcotic predilections, was his stubborn insistence on forming a new, breakaway outfit. I was mystified by this: why work so hard at building up one band only to start again from scratch, and with a decidedly sub-standard combo at that? Surely now he should be enjoying the fruits of his labours?

Babyshambles was born out of those early solo guerrilla gigs. I suspect Pete figured he might as well give it a name and get a loose aggregation of people to back him up in making it more official. Mick from Finley Quaye's band and I offered our services but we were overlooked in favour of 'Scarborough' Steve and his pal, the ludicrously monikered Neil Thunders (not got quite the same ring as Johnny has it?). I think Pete chose to work with them as they were yes-men who would offer no opposition and allow him the kind of autocracy he felt he'd never have in The Libertines. I like Steve and Neil but, at that time, their musicianship was, quite frankly, well beneath the standard required and their 'I Don't Think So' was a shocking display of songwriting.

'SCARBOROUGH' STEVE: "Pete came round to Gunter Grove, and he said he was looking for a guitarist, bassist and drummer. I just jumped on it and said, 'Well Pete, why don't I sing, you play guitar, and we'll get Neil on bass and Max on drums because we're all down here,' and he seemed to be into that.

"The Babyshambles thing for me is a touchy subject because I still think to this day I should be singing for Babyshambles. I could have done that. I sorted out gigs, the two nights at the Troubadour where Pete walked off. All right, we hadn't rehearsed hardly any that week, it was really ropey. We'd all been smoking too many drugs, it just wasn't going right."

PETE: "Babyshambles started in Teesdale Street with the Wolfman and a digital recorder. We recorded the original Babyshambles sessions; 'Black Boy Lane', 'Don't Look Back Into The Sun' and 'I Love You But You're Green'. Then I decided to start The Libertines again with Steve and Neil and Max, three Yorkshiremen – t'Libertines. But people were refusing to book t'Libertines as The Libertines so one promoter had called us Babyshambles because that was the first song in the set."

CARL: "How that all started . . . We had started doing a session in New York, recording, and we were doing very well but then Pete started to invite all his entourage into the studio, all his new friends who all seemed for some reason to have crack in common, or smack or whatever.

"I started to back away and wasn't having it. Peter wanted to call it 'Babyshambles' and I didn't like the name. I didn't want to call it Babyshambles at all. I thought that bore no relevance to anything, apart from Pete's shambles. So anyway, I pulled out of the session and in true Pete style he didn't seem to have any sense of compromise. Rather than see why I'd pulled out he just thought I was wrong and would do it anyway, and decided to call our session with a bunch of stuff I wrote on it 'Babyshambles' and subsequently his band, so that's where that all came from."

By now, Pete was totally estranged from the Libs, even being turned away from the Carling Festival in Leeds by his own security. The rest of the band made a subdued performance on *Top Of The Pops* in what should have been a joyous affirmation that they had firmly cracked the mainstream pop market. 'Don't Look Back Into The Sun', easily their best work to date, was all over the radio. It should have been the time of Pete Doherty's life.

PETE: "I was removed by force from my flat, or somebody else's flat, and taken, again by force to a so-called safe house to stop me going to the festival, but one of my escorts was foolish enough to get out and use a phone-box. He had a few troubles with the phone-box so the other fella jumped out. I was supposed to be asleep – quick as a flash I jumped in the front of the car and I was away, with the intention of getting to Reading. They'd been paid by Rough Trade as 'rehabilitators', in actual fact their sole duty was to keep me away from Paris initially and then the rest of the tour. Unfortunately I wasn't quick-witted enough and was outwitted by the gearbox – fucked the car up. They took advantage of that and I got a kicking – the first of a few. Got held upside down on the Essex Road, they were looking for two grand but 50 pence fell out."

There seemed to be no getting through to Pete – the drugs had a hold on him – but in classic junkie denial everyone could see this but the kid himself. The prospect of imminent fatherhood didn't seem to register either, and whenever I saw him he appeared confused, bitter and manic. In what was seen as a long overdue step, the only option was rehab.

JAMES ENDEACOTT: "We put Pete into rehab in Surrey, a place where a friend of ours had been helped called Farm Place, and after a few conversations, he said, 'OK, I'll go.' Geoff and Jeanette drove Pete down there and I got a phone call from a nurse that night saying he's got no clothes and that I needed to bring him some clothes down. I went into Primark in Lewisham [*laughs*] and spent about a hundred quid on socks, underwear and T-shirts, jogging pants and stuff.

"I drove down there and they said, 'You know you're not allowed to see him?' and I said, 'OK, that's fine,' but as I was dropping the stuff off Pete walked through reception and saw me, and came to sit next to me. The nurse said, 'You've got one minute,' and I was with him for literally one minute. I just saw a man who had had the world taken away from him. He lasted a week – he got a phone call saying Pete Wolf was getting married or something. It was all a scam to get him out. But I remember leaving him that day and driving down the road, I had to stop because I just broke down in tears. I'd just seen this kid, this friend of mine and he was just *hollow*. He didn't want to be there, he was doing it to please everybody else."

GEOFF TRAVIS: "Our reaction to Pete getting himself into drug difficulties was to say to him, 'Peter, sort yourself out, let's just stop everything.' I thought, 'What's important here? It's not making money, or selling records. It's to try and get this young man's life back on track.'"

LISA MOORISH: "We were all quite hysterically concerned and between me, Banny and Pete's sister Amy we called his Mum over and I drove her to that little hotel in Paddington where he always stays. We'd been slowly trying to talk him round into getting some sort of treatment, which he seemed to be going for – this was two weeks before I was due to have our baby. I rang Rough Trade and told Jeanette we were all beside ourselves with worry, and between us we manipulated an 'intervention' – he was due at Rough Trade for a meeting about his Babyshambles project and when he got there he was taken off to rehab. I assumed that he was going to be all right, but little did I know that his usual cronies were phoning up trying to get him out, and of course he was out after six days."

CARL: "Rehab never works the first time anyway. I've seen this situation unfold with many people in my past, which is probably what made me so fearful of Pete's path and kept me at bay from taking that same path myself. First rehab seldom ever works but serves as what they call an intervention, whereby the problem is first addressed as a problem in the person's mind who doesn't even think they've got a problem, it's the first inkling of an awakening to that being the case."

Pete threw himself headlong into the fledgling Babyshambles, the only available outlet for his precocious talent. Gigs were arranged, some of which were somewhat perversely on the same nights his erstwhile band were appearing at much bigger venues. All manner of yes-men, dealers and vultures were descending on an increasingly fragile Pete and there seemed little prospect of a reconciliation with Carl in the near future.

Though aptly shambolic in their organisation, Babyshambles gigs were well-attended affairs. Some gigs ended in brawls, while the second of a two-night stand at The Troubadour Club in Kensington began and ended with Pete bolting up the stairs and out of the building midway through the opening number. The first night had hardly run smoothly either. Pete had invited me up to join him on 'Hooligans On E'. A mass stage invasion ensued with some heavy-handed jostling from the bouncers. Someone smashed me over the head with a particularly weighty microphone and the next thing I knew I was being carried out of the venue, my feet pedalling the air cartoon-style. Out on the kerb I was shooting my mouth off, vowing revenge on the doormen when I noticed blood running down my forehead.

An elderly Geordie lady was kindly dabbing at my head with a hanky while a younger Liverpudlian woman tried to placate me with, "Calm down Peter, yer bleedin'." It was Pete's nan and mum respectively. They were waiting outside as it had been too loud for them inside. I've spoken to Pete's mum on a few occasions and I'm always amazed at how she retains a sense of humour and perspective with the hell she's been put through. She once told me that the Doherty family had spent some time in Swansea. I asked if her son was conceived there as I thought that might explain a few things!

It was in the early days of Pete's estrangement from the rest of The Libertines that I decided to put some distance between myself and my increasingly erratic chum – to preserve my credibility as well as my health. Obviously he was my main friend from the band but I liked and respected all of them. So when I got wind that Carl and the others were frowning upon the company Pete was keeping I was anxious not to be lumped in with them.

Late one night Pete unexpectedly showed up at my flat. I hadn't seen him for a while and he appeared to have undergone a total image change. He'd shaved his head of his shaggy indie-kid locks, was wearing a claret-and-blue Fred Perry polo shirt, drainpipe jeans and Reebok trainers. All that was missing were the Doc Marten boots and his metamorphosis into Tim Roth's character from *Made In Britain* would have been complete.

As well as the new look, Pete had recently acquired a number of new "mates" and he took me round to visit one of them, just a short walk from my own flat. Climbing the steps of a rundown estate I should have known what was coming but still I wasn't prepared for what I was to see. Pete's new mate was the proprietor of a full-on crack den. As soon as I walked in I wished I'd stayed at home with *Coronation Street*. All sorts of deadbeats were coming and going and a woman was injecting into her groin in a corner of the room. Charming. I was invited to sit on the bed but declined as it was covered with needles. It was clear Pete and his new pals had become fast friends around a communal glass dick. I couldn't get out of there quickly enough. I've seen a few things in my time but this was totally depressing. Given the nature of the drug some drop-outs were showing serious signs of psychosis and this added a tangible air of danger, an occupational hazard in that sort of place.*

A few hours later Pete was back on my doorstep. We sat up for

---

* A month or so later this *des res* was all over the front page of the *Camden New Journal* and the proprietors behind bars.

the rest of the night playing guitars and watching films. Pete was transfixed by Sam Peckinpah's *Straw Dogs* but kept nodding out during the Factory Records' flick *24 Hour Party People* – ironic as the lifestyle he was now leading made Shaun Ryder and Bez's antics seem like the teddy bear's picnic.

When I left for a week's holiday in Crete I was philosophical about Pete. He was in bad shape, totally polarised from the rest of The Libertines and getting further out by the day. I honestly despaired for him, and wondered what news I'd return home to. The night before I went away he'd turned up at my flat on a lovely pillar-box red Vespa, *sans* helmet, asking for a 300 quid loan. I couldn't say no as he knew I had it to lend and he'd have done the same for me, but I made sure I accompanied him to the band's accountants in Baker Street to get it back. He skipped down the steps with pre-cisely ten times what he owed me, whacking himself on the head with the wedge of notes maniacally, like a kid about to *buy* the sweetshop. I had to get out of the taxi at Regent's Park as Pete was cock-a-hoop, whooping with joy on his way to his dealers via a tattooist. Needless to say the bread was long gone by the following day and I understand he also wrote off the scooter somewhere along the way.

EDDIE PILLER (ACID JAZZ RECORDS): "I'd heard he'd bought a lovely little Vespa 50 from the Scooter Emporium in Brick Lane. Apparently his record company bought it for him. He had it about two weeks then brought it back asking if they'd buy it back off him. My mate who runs the place told him, 'Nah, we sell, not buy.' Well after some frantic negotiating he ended up taking peanuts for it, 200 quid or something silly. He used to come into my shop, The Soul Kitchen on Bethnal Green Road, fairly regularly just after he got his deal and he must have bought five or six 1960's re-conditioned battery-operated record players, for over a ton a time. He was really polite, really cool. What can I say? He looked like a Mod, of course I liked him. I was sorry to hear he was having problems."

My Greek getaway was quiet and uneventful, just what the doctor ordered, until the last night when I got so shit-faced on ouzo and brandy that airport officials stopped me boarding the flight home. Attempting a mercy dash through customs for the runway made matters worse and I was left at the airport waving my mate Mick off to Gatwick, under threat of arrest. I spent the next three days sleeping on the beach until I could get another flight home. To kill time I spent many hours in an internet café on the seafront. Having no phone numbers of friends, the site became something of a lifeline, and I even sent out a jokey SOS to Pete directly, prompting a reply which really lifted my spirits. Perversely, within Pete's communiqué was a line which read, "If your flatmate speaks to you first, I wasn't trying to burgle you." Confused, I rang my flatmate Mark to see if he could shed any light on Pete's cryptic dispatch. He was loath to tell me what had happened but eventually he did, and as it unfolded a grim sequence of events left me totally crushed.

Only the night before, at about 1 a.m., Mark had heard an incessant ringing of the doorbell. He'd ignored it but when getting up to get a cold drink he was totally spooked by the sight of a ghoulish apparition at the kitchen window. It was Pete. When asked what he was doing in our back garden at such an ungodly hour, Pete informed Mark that he was looking for me, knowing full well I was thousands of miles away. Unwittingly Mark let him in the back door and promptly out the front. On being told this, it slowly dawned on me that Pete had attempted the unthinkable – to roll me over! I put the phone down and cut a swathe through the crowds of holiday revellers to a quiet spot on a pier. In a bit of a daze I plonked myself down and tried to kid myself that there could be another reason for Pete being in my back garden. Of course, there wasn't and it hit me like a ton of bricks. For the first time since my hero Joe Strummer died I wept, wondering how the hell it had come to this.

I woke on the beach the next day, stark naked and covered in mosquito bites, trying to come to terms with this diabolical liberty. I was filled with a mixture of fury and sadness.

When I got back to the UK, I'd calmed down enough to plot what I was going to do with the boy wonder. I didn't want to go on the warpath and annihilate him, I'd far sooner think it was all a terrible misunderstanding. Then I took a phone call from Lisa and as I was deliberating over whether to tell her my suspicions she removed all doubt from my mind.

LISA MOORISH: "I'd just had the baby, which he turned up for and was, well, I won't say fine but it was what it was. It was great that he was there for the birth but at that point he was really low, he was really bad. Then he just disappeared and I didn't hear from him for a week. I was hysterical, breast-feeding, in a right state. Day five or six I get hold of him and ask, 'Where have you been? I've been worried, etc., etc.,' and he says, 'Look, you may not see me for a couple of years,' sounding really dramatic. I sort of panicked and said, 'What do you mean?' 'Oh, I've done something really bad.' 'Like what?' 'I've burgled Carl's flat, kicked the door in.' He didn't really say why, he sounded pretty gone but he obviously wanted to get it off his chest. I was devastated, I told him to get round here now and sort it out but he wouldn't come.

"I rang his sister, saying, 'What shall we do?' I suggested we ring the police, because it was so outrageous. I was worried about his state of mind and thought if he's arrested they can at least look after him. I almost didn't believe him so Amy and I went round to Carl's place and sure enough the door was kicked in. We went in and it wasn't that messy but we could see it had been disturbed. Carl was away in Japan and I thought, 'Shit, it's on me now, I can't shirk my responsibility.' I think Amy offered to do it but I said, 'No, it's not fair, it's me he told and I don't mind telling him to his face that I've done this because I'm doing it for the right reasons.'

"So I called the police, it was a really upsetting experience. Pete was arrested and he knew instantly it was me because I was on the police report, and I wasn't going to deny it anyway. I didn't go to court. He was saying, 'Lisa Moorish grassed me up,' and Amy was, like, 'Look Peter, you rang her and told her.' I thought it was a bit of a cry for help, but I thought he'd understand a lot more than he did at the time but he was very, very angry for a long time. He felt I'd let him down."

CARL: "I got to the airport coming back off tour and I was supposed to be going to see this new girl and I was really excited, couldn't wait because it had been so hard in Japan, you know I didn't *want* to tour without Pete and those early days it hurt *so much*. I can't see how Pete can be in any more pain than me, and thinking that he's got some paranoid suspicion that I'm just lording it up, enjoying myself . . . it was kind of a hellish time for me.

"So I came back and I thought that my respite, my sanctuary was going to be this romance detached from everything else. On getting to the airport and turning my phone on I get a message from Banny saying your flat's been broken into, so obviously I was worried about my sister Lucy who was unwell and living in the flat at the time, but the one thing I wanted to do was escape from it all with a young romance and disappear up North, and I couldn't do that. It was like a nightmare and you wake up and you're still dreaming, it's another nightmare – you know that feeling? I was so worried about the way Pete was behaving anyway. Everyone wanted to know he was safe. I was never shocked, just disappointed."

JAMES ENDEACOTT: "I was camping in Oxfordshire with my family and Lisa called me and told me Pete's broken into Carl's flat. I knew that just before he'd been in trouble, he'd been trying to smash a bank up or something and he'd nicked a car, he was so out of control. I just thought, 'Fucking hell.' My initial reaction was one I didn't want and I didn't like it, but I was *relieved* that Pete was going to prison because he was pushing the self-destruct button and you didn't know where it was going to end. Every day it was something else. Everyone was upset but Carl was *really* upset, really hurt."

ROGER SARGENT: "I was *livid*, when I found out. I was really upset, I couldn't believe that he'd done it; it was one of the most shocking things that I've ever heard. At Reading and Leeds it was really tense. The thing I remember about all those gigs without Pete is how angsty and angry Carl was."

It turned out the burglary happened the same Friday that Pete had dropped in on my place. When I heard Pete was showing no remorse, I registered my outrage and disgust on The Libertines official website that when I caught up with him he'd meet an army of me. I'd just come into a lump of cash and set about obliterating it within days of my return, finding getting smashed was the best way of dealing with this betrayal.

I soon straightened out and decided to call Carl who was understandably dazed with all that had gone on but was also livid that his sister could have been there when Pete came calling. As usual I couldn't understand what he was saying down the phone so a meeting was arranged. I spoke to John who didn't have much sympathy as he'd warned me to stop getting into mischief with his singer a few months earlier and of course I hadn't heeded it. Carl's solicitor got in contact and we colluded over getting a strong case against Pete. I couldn't go through with it and as no actual crime had been committed against me it would have been pointless to throw my lot in anyway.

The situation was complicated by a pre-arranged American tour which the band couldn't get out of.

JAMES ENDEACOTT: "Carl didn't want to go but at the same time I think he wanted to get away from it all. Nobody really wanted to do it, but they did OK with the new guy Anthony. It was not what anybody wanted. It was all there in the palm of their hand with the single 'Don't Look Back Into The Sun', it was all there and it just seemed to be falling apart."

CHAPTER 7

What A Waste

I ARRIVED at The Depot rehearsal facility after a heavy afternoon's drinking and though I was pleased to see the guys, the atmosphere was anything but jolly. That night's rehearsal would be my only chance to see the band before they were heading off across the Atlantic, the following day, for nearly three weeks.

A measure of how far they'd come in such a short space of time was their surroundings in Studio One, a vast, football-pitch sized room used by the likes of Oasis and big-name US bands when they were in town. Supplemented by new boy Anthony Rossomando, the new-look Libertines created a sound akin to a runaway train; it was the biggest, fullest sound I'd heard from them. I sat on the floor with a can of Stella Artois and listened to the band go through 15 or so songs. Each one sounded like a classic, and they were still barely a year old. The new kid was technically better than Pete and he certainly looked good; all hair and skinny New York chic. Throwing classic rock shapes he looked like an amalgam of all five Strokes. But he wasn't Pete Doherty.

It was good to see Carl, John and Gary even if it was under such strange circumstances, and I felt a great sense of admiration, for Carl especially, trooping on stubbornly in the face of such adversity. I found Anthony very personable, with his "dude!"-style jive he was like Bill and Ted rolled into one. He'd put his band in New York, The Damn Personals, on hold to step into Pete's shoes at short notice. Rehearsal over, Carl and I repaired to the nearby New-market Tavern to discuss everything that had gone down and to offer each other a little mutual support. It was hard to believe he hadn't seen his old partner for two months or so, and when I showed him a photo of a freshly shorn Pete, he scarcely recognised him. The recent weeks' events had clearly taken a toll, and chain-smoking anxiously, Carl looked shattered in every sense.

During the course of our talk, he poured his heart out. I was under no illusions as we had never been the best of pals but I felt we shared a mutual respect for one another. Carl vented his spleen on just about everybody whom he considered to have played a part in Pete's demise, reserving extra vitriol for 'Scarborough' Steve, up until then a valued friend of equal standing with both Pete and Carl. I knew he didn't hate Steve, but he lashed out with the wounded and confused rationale of a spurned lover. Of course it was with this passion and fire that he'd captivated The Libertines' audience, the polar opposite of Pete's stubborn idealism, and while I dug both, I really felt for Carl.

Never a guy to need his arm twisted for a night out, and dis-regarding his early morning call for the airport, we jumped into a cab and headed for The Columbia Hotel in Queensway where visit-ing US band, The Hiss were supposedly having a shindig. While stopping off at Carl's Baker Street pad, I surveyed the damage to the front door. "Real pro job, eh?" Carl said half-jokingly, though neither of us managed more than a wry frown.

TONY LINKIN: "I couldn't believe it had really happened. Carl was very laid-back, I mean, he was upset that his mate would break into his house but he seemed to be more upset about his sister than his material goods. His sister was so distressed that he had to back her up."

GEOFF TRAVIS: "I didn't really understand what was going on; why Carl was bringing charges I don't know, it seemed a bit extreme but on the other hand I thought maybe it'll be good for [Pete]. If he can't stay in rehab for ten seconds then perhaps jail will be good."

I was in the middle of another bender I didn't want to stop and I wasn't thinking straight. The night after I saw Carl I decided I would phone Pete. I demanded a credible explanation as to what he was doing in my garden that night, but unable to provide one and heavily slurring, he went on the offensive, goading me that he could burgle me any time he fancied. I couldn't believe what I was hearing and being confused and angry, I decided on a course of tough justice. By now, there were plenty who felt Pete needed to be brought into line but no one had put themselves up for the job. I took a cab to the White City address he'd been bailed to, burst through the door and up the stairs, catching Pete *in flagrante*. Quick as a shot he was up, hastily pulling on his jeans and Converse boots (both, perversely, borrowed a few weeks earlier from yours truly), saying, "OK, but it's not my gaff so let's do it in the street."

I allowed him a head start which he used to his advantage by clearing three flights of stairs in three giant leaps. Outside I watched incredulously as he ran over a parked car to make good his escape. I caught up with him and thumped him a few times, explaining all the while that this was in retribution. I think this sank in and knowing that I was never going to really hurt him, he took those punches in the spirit they were thrown. A few of his hangers-on ran out, half-dressed, screaming for me to stop, and with the neighbours' lights turning on and people coming out to see what was afoot, threatening to call the law, I slipped away into the night.

I woke the next day and it registered right away: I'd given my good mate a moderate kicking. I lay in bed weighing it up. Granted, there was some justification as many said he had it coming, but I felt rotten. I was relieved when I was told that Pete had posted a dispatch on his own Babyshambles website describing the previous night's events, accepting his punishment, and apologising to me. To this day Pete still says he deserved it but, jokes aside, I certainly didn't enjoy doing it.

The week immediately after his arrest in August 2003 the *NME* showed a shaven-headed Pete sticking two fingers up to the cameras outside Horseferry Magistrates Court. It was pure Gallagher-esque behaviour but the sallow complexion and empty eyes belied any notion that this show of defiance was swaggering bravado. Even his most optimistic admirers would have had to admit that Pete looked like he was suffocating under the weight of his own celebrity.

The ensuing weeks saw more confusion. This varied from Pete declaring he was in a new band (called The Libertines!), to frank admissions in the *Evening Standard*: "Yes I'm a heroin addict, yes I'm addicted to crack cocaine and I don't know what to do." When he let slip, "I need a good kicking," it further eased my conscience for the action I'd taken a week earlier. Indeed many people close to him had actually thanked me for pursuing that course of action, though this was the last thing I wanted. Like everybody else, all I wanted was to see Pete beat his demons and get back to normality.

Meanwhile, Carl, John and Gary, supplemented by Anthony, fulfilled their summer tour obligations. Their Glastonbury appearance, which should have been a crystallisation of the previous five years slog, was described as "missing the spirit and passion" and of Carl making "the best of a bad job" in a set during which there were lengthy periods where it fell flat. Babyshambles weren't faring much better in the critical acclaim stakes. A review of the Troubadour Café gig was less than complimentary; "too painful for words" said one hack in succinct summation. It was only 14 months since The Libertines had adorned the cover of the *NME* for the first time, with Pete in a vintage England football shirt, looking fat-faced and playful; the Babyshambles review carried a picture of 'Scarborough'

Steve barking into the mic with a painfully thin, bare-chested Pete backing him up on guitar, looking more battered than the straw trilby covering his shaven head.

Pete's court case took place at Horseferry Road Magistrates Court, Westminster, on September 8. I toyed with the idea of attending but stayed away knowing it would be a circus. When Pete turned up in a beige mac, trilby and a smirk for the cameras, the district judge Roger Davies took a dim view of his capricious demeanour. In summing up, he said, "[Doherty] probably was suddenly earning too much money for his age and began behaving irresponsibly. Unlike most of us who have to study and work hard, they suddenly acquire wealth." The beak's self-righteous tone continued: "[Doherty] continues to pursue a hedonistic lifestyle which involves heavy use of drugs," concluding with him handing down a sentence of six months. As his solicitor Richard Locke announced he would be launching an "immediate appeal", Pete was taken down.

PETE: "Alan McGee was the only person who said, 'You're gonna go to prison.' We ended up at my sister's house a week before the hearing and he just said, 'I think you'll go down.' I took what he said quite seriously, but not thought for a second that he might be right."

TONY LINKIN: "I never thought he'd go to prison, I thought it had all been blown out of proportion. The last thing Carl wanted was to see him put in prison but they couldn't drop the charges because it was a police charge. Also, we were all wise enough to know that that wasn't necessarily the best place for him."

ROGER SARGENT: "I was on a beach in Greece and got a text saying that Pete had been sent down and it was really upsetting, despite what he'd done. I mean, you never like to hear of any of your mates going to prison."

JAMES ENDEACOTT: "I felt so bad for him because I knew he didn't want to be there, I knew he'd find it hard; he isn't built for that world. We weren't really thinking about the band, we just wanted Pete to be better, didn't want him to die; whenever the phone went at seven or eight in the morning I thought it would be someone telling me he'd gone. Rough Trade didn't care if the band never made another record again."

PETE: "I was so happy to get out. I mean, a packet of crisps was a fucking luxury. In the open prison I managed to get the chaplain to borrow me a guitar but not in Wandsworth. When I did get hold of one it was unbelievable, because it had been two weeks or something but it seemed like an eternity. I played 'Don't Look Back Into The Sun' to myself and I wept. It was just an old standard acoustic, had a couple of stickers on it. I remember thinking when I played the guitar, I'm going to put it *all behind me*, and start again with Carl. I couldn't wait to play with him.

"Prison's a funny place, there's a lot of attitude and a lot of negativity as well. You become very self-conscious in a way, especially in the open prison where you are allowed, in some cases, to leave your cell. There's a lot of tension as well, it kicks off all the time. It becomes very territorial with a lot of fear. On the surface it seemed to be cleaner, and you had more freedom but there was something a bit more secure about Wandsworth. Technically there's nothing stopping you getting over the fence at the open prison and hopping it. It's full of prisoners from Wormwood Scrubs, Wandsworth and Brixton.

"I shouldn't have been in Wandsworth because I was only a Category D prisoner and it's an A Category prison, but there were a lot more long-term hardcore criminals, and there was some kind of, not *community*, but *standing*. Even like being in the dinner queue in the open prison was hard work; if another prisoner read this they'd think I was a complete fucking lunatic, but it was a real shock to the system. I was scared and very paranoid. You're put in such close confines with one other individual and it's pot luck really. Wandsworth is really dingy, and dirty, and Victorian, with pigeons and rats – rats *everywhere*. Hundreds and hundreds of men in little rooms, all that food getting lobbed out of windows. They revel in their bad name, the overcrowding, the lack of positive outlets for people's energy. A lot of people can't read or write, or speak English, with no skills or training.

"The majority of the screws make it their duty to make it as difficult for you as possible, though from what I learnt off the other prisoners it's changed dramatically in the last five years for the better. The screws used to give you *right kickings*, a proper old-school discipline. Now it's different because you've got privatisation of the prison guards. I was getting a ridiculous amount of mail and they didn't like that, they got really annoyed and they held things back; things that I know I should have got but I didn't.

"I got a smack in the mouth in the first few days but then the fella who did it kind of embraced me which was a bit strange. I had another fella looking over my shoulder trying to get my PIN number on my phone card which is a big thing in prisons, but someone was looking out for me by then, a guy with dreadlocks who held him up against a wall and said, 'What the fuck are you doing?' so I noticed a hierarchy right away. For some reason some people had a bit more freedom than others. One day I passed out in the dinner queue of the open prison, fell unconscious and dropped forward. A fella caught me by the back of my shirt before I smashed my face in. I just lost consciousness through lack of nutrition because you don't get hardly anything to eat.

"I didn't smoke a single pipe of crack while I was in there but for weed, hash and heroin I managed to make connections pretty quickly, got into a little bit of bother with someone. I told someone on the outside to drop some money off to a fella in Peckham and in turn I'd get something on tic. It all went wrong and suddenly I'm gonna get my legs broken, but then I get moved to the open prison, owing money, but then I got moved *back* to Wandsworth. Fortunately a few phone calls were made and it was all resolved.

"The screws don't turn a blind eye to drug use, and there's piss tests every five minutes. At first I had to completely cut down, with no medication but I think the psychological shock of being in prison overrode any withdrawal. There was no exercise, though once I had the chance of a game of football but by that time I was glad to have the cell to myself for half an hour. I was banged up for 23 hours a day at Wandsworth. There's supposed to be a library [*laughs*]. It's hard to describe exactly how insanely boring it was. I remember when I was a kid boredom was forbidden, the use of the word boring was a real bad thing – my dad wouldn't have it. I said it once and I never said it again. I think looking back I made very good use of the time – at the open prison I wrote 'Tomblands' and read some wonderful books, the Stuart Sutcliffe biography, *Crime And Punishment* by Dostoevsky which was amazing.

"I think intensive brain surgery can change someone's personality or an individual's make-up, and certain experiences maybe like seeing a ghost or coming back from the dead can change your life and your personality forever. Otherwise, people are pretty much set in their ways, especially once they surpass their early twenties, but *the severity of a punishment* has never been proven in any society or any system of justice to affect the likelihood of re-offending – it's been proven systematically. Prison as I experienced it serves to frustrate the individual, to breed resentment and full-on antagonism.

"At the open prison my nan and sister came to visit, and Lisa with the baby but I couldn't wait to get back to the cell. I felt really ugly and dirty. I wasn't really prepared; I know some people may see one month as a bit of a cushy ride but one month, one minute, one year? I'd have made an escape attempt from the open prison if I'd been there much longer. People were running off all the time. I tried to arrange it with someone to bring a van down to the Isle of Sheppey.

"Just before I was released I remember being sat on a bunk staring at the wall where I'd tried to scrub out this swastika but it was scraped in with a nail. I'd been having a little bit of banter with my cellmate, in the end he just hopped down and said, 'Listen mate, with all the best will in the world, Pete, you're gonna be *straight back* on that pipe as soon as you get out of here – and there's only one place it leads to, only one outcome, death or mathematics.' They were the circumstances I was in, unable to get crack, and opening up to somebody who didn't know my story, but he just saw the facts, and that I had a successful future ahead of me with or without The Libertines, but if I chose that path, I was gonna fuck it up. But after that period of abstinence and suffering I wanted to give myself a little treat."

Later, Pete's jail term and his subsequent reconciliation with The Libertines put paid to that line-up of Babyshambles and, along with it, Steve and Neil's aspirations of rock stardom. Hopefully, rock'n' roll's fickle finger of fate may yet prod Steve in the direction he wants.

CHAPTER 8

Back From The Dead

TO everyone's relief Pete was released early in October 2003, his sentence reduced from six months to two. His defence counsel told the appeal hearing, "[Doherty] is a 24-year-old who had suddenly come into a bit of fame and a bit of money and clearly has a drug habit," adding that his actions had been "unplanned and impulsive."

Pete was curious as to why I hadn't been in touch but I didn't want to send him a letter that would be lost among a load of fawning fan mail. He was being lauded in the press and by Libertines' fans as some sort of people's hero, a kind of modern day Robin Hood. Conversely, Carl was the subject of contemptuous whispering in some circles as if he was the villain of the piece, which I found both bizarre and unjust. The whole of the law was Pete had burgled his best mate and there's fuck all romantic or celebratory about that. I felt the fact that it was all being played out weekly in the *NME* to be a real tragedy.

Tellingly, Carl also didn't contact Pete while he was in jail.

CARL: "I wanted to write him a letter. I think I wrote him a post-card actually. It was the hardest thing I've ever written. He wrote me a couple of letters but he just seemed off his nut."

Similarly when Pete came out everyone wanted a piece of him and I wanted no part in that charade either. While it would be a few weeks before I saw him, his old mate was there at the prison gates.

CARL: "It was fucking hard for me to go to that prison; it's hard to get up at six in the morning. It wasn't easy for me to fucking do that and then to see all the *NME* and that waiting outside and to not know what the fuck I was gonna find. Essentially it was joyful that we could get back together, put it all behind us. Everyone had their own take on it, everyone said, 'Oh, I wouldn't ever bother seeing him again.' We both had that."

TONY LINKIN: "Carl went down to meet Pete from prison. He was very, very scared going down there because he wasn't sure how Pete would react to seeing him outside the gate. Roger didn't really want to take any pictures, which is why there aren't that many outside the prison because he felt it was neither the time nor place."

ROGER SARGENT: "We were there from half seven in the morning, and he didn't get out until half eleven. We weren't even in a car, we were just milling about. Carl was very nervous, he really didn't know what to expect. Eventually the big heavy doors opened, it was a bit like *Porridge*, and Pete came walking towards us. They clocked each other and it was all smiles, and hugs and tears. It was great, exactly how you'd want it to be. They wanted some time on their own so they went to this fella Reg's house nearby. You know the shot on the back of the 'Can't Stand Me Now' single? That was taken at Reg's place just after Pete had got out."

PETE: "Yeah, I was pleased to see him but I didn't *for a second* think he'd be there. I didn't really have any doubt in my mind how I'd be with him. I had no intention of blaming him. Something happened towards the last days of prison where I realised, 'Hang on a minute,

I've been a cunt as well, done a few bad things.' I could admit that. *I'm* sorry too, but I didn't expect to see him anyway. It was very emotional. You've got to understand that there was complete elation on my part to be out, *complete* elation. I bought a pack of fags and a can of beer. Carl was a little bit subdued, but then we ended up in a boozer in the West End not far from my accountant's where I'd gone to pick up a few quid which was *amazing*, as you can imagine. We were cracking jokes, a few of them a bit near the knuckle. We spent a good few hours in there, ended up causing a bit of a scene, getting a bit rowdy with cigars and David Niven's we called 'em, which is whisky and ginger beers. Getting pissed together and talking about the future really.

"The plan was to go and see my sister but I stopped off somewhere to score rocks and brown. I think Carl had been clean for a little while, but after what happened between me and him and then prison, I felt different towards Carl. I knew it was still the same but I wanted so badly for it to be all or nothing, wanting it to be me and him. But then I knew that that could not be and that was not what he wanted anyway. I was happy to have Gary and John, and Carl had told me his feelings, he said that having spent time without me with Gary and John he realised that Gary was fucking amazing, really powerful, and he found John a bit annoying but he's just Mr. Lombard isn't he. I fell back into being a little more emotionally dependant on Carl but I realised I had to cut myself off from demanding him like that."

ROGER SARGENT: "I got a couple of calls throughout the day from a progressively drunker Carl, and Peter as well, talking about this gig that Peter was going to do in Chatham that evening. We converged at Victoria and it was just brilliant, a real wave of relief. Carl was fucking *hammered* by this stage – beer, brandy, wine, whisky. He had a little bit of a snooze on the train so he was a bit better by the time we got down there."

TONY LINKIN: "Pete was meant to be doing a gig at the Tap'n'Tin anyway so it was quickly decided that we'd all go down there. We met at Victoria Station, except Pete who had gone off to see his sister, I think. So we got a train down there, Carl was *very* pissed, he was so pleased to see Pete really, but he kept trying to pick a fight with me I seem to recall [*laughs*]. He was so pissed! We were sat in a first-class carriage and he was trying to sleep and every time anyone came by and knocked him he'd go, 'Fucking hell, Tony!' It got to the point where I had to just sit there, quiet as anything. In fact, I'm the one who Roger wrote the 'Pete' and 'Carl' thing on my hands which is in the corner of the picture on the album cover, I've been edited out, but the first thing Carl said was, 'Why have you got Pete written on your *right* hand?' which is sort of typical.

"It was a great night, a fantastic evening. The whole thing had to end though, as usual, with Carl getting rushed off to hospital. He tried jumping over something, I'm not sure what, but he landed on his face basically. He was so pissed in the afternoon I was surprised he did the gig so well. He did the gig amazingly well."

ROGER SARGENT: "Carl jumped on a bollard, slipped and cut his chin. I thought someone had hit him, because he'd said he'd had some jip from the bouncers. He was lying on the floor in a pool of blood so I was like, 'What the fuck happened? Who fucking hit you?' I started running down the street towards the bouncers and Pete's sister came after me going, 'No, no!'" [*laughs*]

JAMES ENDEACOTT: "It was a shambolic gig. If you just heard the audio of it you'd think it was the worst band in the world but it was a great, great night. Carl smashed his face up and Pete grabbed a phone off somebody and called 999, and was hugging him and making sure he was all right and you know, you really thought the world is a better place. There was a lot of love going down and you felt that everything had been forgiven and this is year zero again.

"Pete had got in touch with Alan McGee . . . I think he'd actually asked Alan to manage him while he wasn't in the band but Alan wanted to manage The Libertines."

By the end of September, the band had finished promoting the first album and the time had come to start thinking about the next album. Although Banny was contractually committed to managing them for the second album, she chose to leave, informing the band of her decision in a series of meetings and phone calls. She had been there from the start, and was choosing to leave, just as The Libertines were attracting interest from the national press and selling out their biggest shows to date at the Kentish Town Forum and Manchester Academy. But she was unconvinced that Pete was manageable in his current state and didn't believe things would be different from the chaos of the last few months, unless the day ever came when Pete wanted to change, for himself and on his own terms.

With Pete a free man and a brand new management team at the helm, it marked the start of a new era for The Libertines. The renewed gravitas that came with McGee's involvement tended to diminish the role of Banny Pootschi, who deserves a great deal of credit. She took the band from a feckless bunch of chancers to a deal with Rough Trade and EMI Music Publishing, leaving her job at Warner Records to manage them exclusively for two years by which time she had established the worldwide infrastructure for the band and overseen four steadily progressing Top 40 hit singles, the last being 'Don't Look Back Into The Sun' and the release of *Up The Bracket*. Things certainly would not have happened the way they did or anywhere near as quickly without her work ethic and a high level of professionalism. It's worth remembering that by the time Banny parted company with The Libertines at the end of October 2003, they had sold 100,000 copies of *Up The Bracket* and had just topped *The Guardian*'s 40 Best British Bands poll, beating the likes of Coldplay and Oasis. Still, if anyone in the business had the credentials to deal with "difficult" *artistes* it had to be McGee, having played nursemaid to The Jesus and Mary Chain, My Bloody Valentine, Primal Scream, and Oasis.

PETE: "Alan turned up at the Sony studios when we were mixing the 'Up The Bracket' single and I had had a brief chat with him there. He turned up to see Mick [Jones] who I think he knew and to just have a sniff around. One thing Alan said was he didn't know what went on but how it had got to the stage where I was thrown out of the band was beyond him, and if he was to manage us, it would never happen again. He had the experience and the enthusiasm and the money to get us back on track, give us the confidence and the backing we needed to keep it together. I had complete faith and belief in him, complete trust, and I liked him. Carl got on with him very well – they're both as insane as each other."

CARL: "I think McGee is attracted like a moth to a candle to bands that are in distress. At the same time he's got a big heart, and wanted only to offer help; it wasn't even a preamble to management, he just wanted to help. He came to me and he said, 'I wanna see you back with your buddy,' and 'I know how to deal with drugs in bands better than anyone else in the world,' and I believed him – I still do. I mean, there's only *so much* you can do, but whatever can be done, McGee did it.

"I found him quite hard work, a really daunting character. I'd always heard he was a real bastard so I was surprised when he wasn't, and just assumed he was holding back from being a bastard but no, he wasn't, he was a genuinely loveable fella with an all-round character. *Instantly* mimicable but that's always good anyway."

LISA MOORISH: "I'd been telling Pete for about six months to give Alan a call, just for some advice because he'd kind of been there, seen it, done it and finally after about six months of me asking, he did. At the same time I was on the phone to Carl in America saying, 'Look, why don't you give Alan a ring?', because those two weren't speaking, there was no mediation and the gap was widening. I just saw an opportunity to go in as a mate of them both, though I kept it quiet from each one what I was doing."

Shortly after, Carl and Pete retreated to Alan's house on the Welsh borders to rest, write and generally become reacquainted. Predictably, the good ship Albion would quickly sail into familiarly stormy waters.

PETE: "We were in the valleys; sweeping, panoramic views from this Arcadian, Victoriana charabanc of a house. Wooden, three-point-turn staircase, marble steps, old brass beds, high ceilings. A housekeeper comes down, sticks your stuff in the fridge. Beautiful records. It was actually a bit awkward trying to get Carl just to sit with me and strum; when he does I find that he's drinking very heavily, drinking quickly, and it's whisky. He actually said, 'Don't let me drink this,' but I do. First day I woke and found Carl and Alan had gone down to the local town, the one with all the books . . . Hay-on-Wye, that's it. Comes back with some lovely little books. Carl was trying to get Alan to sort out a local coke dealer but it wasn't happening. I'd brought a little something with me, that Carl was unaware of, but it was really nothing to write home about and so it quickly disappeared and I was just filled with this enthusiasm. 'What Became Of The Likely Lads?' was born.

"That night in Wales was the first time we'd spoken openly, heartfelt, passionately and in the end with a temper, about how we felt about each other, talking with accusative tones. It fell into the old-fashioned Carl and Pete vibe but I'm talking about before being signed, I'm talking about when we were stranded together in oblivion, in skanky little basements fighting over the last cigarette, when we would get nasty, and it got nasty again. He started saying, 'I

141

suffered too,' and I said, 'Well yeah, I know,' and then all these mad confessions came out of him. He'd sat on the back of the tour bus filling himself with everything, brown, crack, loads of coke and he just didn't give a fuck – and this is what really disturbed me, it occurred to me that he was taking the things that I was not allowed back in the band for taking!"

CARL: "We pretty much just dashed straight off to Wales to live in a fucking house together. What kind of recipe for disaster was that? After all that, there was the reason we broke up in the first place that had to come out eventually, so that's why I fucking trashed my face in. Pete went to bed, and I just looked at myself in the mirror and that's what kind of disgusted me. I was on my own in the bathroom completely pissed, in this situation that I didn't know how it had happened, but knowing that I hadn't done anything wrong *really*, and I managed to conjure up all this hate out of nowhere and [I had] become a hated person in some respects, and I just fucking belted my face as many times as I could against the sink."

PETE: "He starts crying, he starts smashing shit up. Remember this is Alan's house, a really nice house. He's been prone to doing that sort of thing before but never in someone's house, it's almost unbelievable what I'm seeing. I'm quite aggressive, and I'm quite fit so I know I can have him because he's a wreck but I just try to sit him down so I grab him. I hadn't drunk much, but he had. He pushes me, he calls me a cunt, says he wishes I was dead."

TONY LINKIN: "Alan McGee got involved pretty much straight after Pete came out of prison and took them down to Wales. It kicked off one night, it was just two very drunk people arguing at four in the morning. It was all made up very, very quickly. Carl didn't mean to hurt himself as much as he did, because he almost lost the sight in one eye and God knows what else, it was awful really."

PETE: "In the morning him and Alan walked into my room, he's wearing his big old blue crombie, hair all over the place and the most horrific fucking scene I've ever seen in my life. Alan goes, 'Did you do this?' That's what I woke up to. I think he's mucking about, like he's got a joke-shop thing on his face. Scary, it was. Carl was stood there quiet, completely in shock. Then it clicks that it's real and I'm like, 'Oh my God, oh my God.' After they went to the hospital I thought, 'What the fuck *has* happened?' I thought Alan had done it. Carl knew all along but he couldn't say it, then he finally admitted it to the doctor because they were gonna come and investigate, because he had, like, 80 stitches in his face. It really was fucking serious. And so that put paid to the writing holiday. I'll never really know what Alan thought. From that moment on nothing was ever, *ever* the same. Things had returned to that creative bickering, a little bit of spite but a *lot* of love . . . and then that happened, and for the next month I couldn't see him, Annalisa was nursing him, he couldn't leave his flat. His sister was there so I wasn't allowed there. One time I was at Rough Trade I decided I was going to see him, Annalisa said, 'No, he's asleep.' I said, 'I don't fucking *care*, he's my friend, he's my best friend and I'm coming to see him whether he's asleep or not,' but she said no.

"For the first time ever he paid the price for it. Things he's done before where he's escaped, walking on things that are too high and not dying, throwing himself in harbours when he can't swim."

ALAN McGEE: "They're the most extreme band I've ever worked with. It's sort of not rock'n'roll. I don't know what it is. Mental illness, probably."

After his release Pete took up residence in a shoebox of a flat in Whitechapel. It was a right shithole on a council estate tucked behind The Blind Beggar. Of course it suited him down to the ground. I think he enjoyed the Dickensian vibe of the area, and it was handy for nicking from Sainsbury's (supermarket) too. You could barely swing a cat in there but pretty soon it became gig-central, though personally I never attended any. I heard reports that upwards of 30 were squeezing in some nights.

After the initial kiss-and-make-up in Chatham and the debacle at Alan's pad in Wales, Pete and Carl changed the location to France in an attempt to get the creative juices flowing and their friendship back on track.

CARL: "We went to Paris. I wanted to go *with Pete*, we had a lot of work to do as friends, and as writers, and I wanted to get Pete away from the *crowd*, first and foremost, and secondly the *drugs*. It could have been Paris, it could have been Beirut, it could have been Easter Island, just anywhere with four walls and curtains you could close, and something you could sit on and play your guitar and write. A lot of time was spent just sleeping, in this grotty hotel room next to the Sexodrome on the Pigalle. We had a lot of good times, drunk, up and down the Pigalle. One night we went to the Sexodrome and verbalised that we wanted to see the sex show, or peep show, and so this moth-eaten old bint behind the counter charged us our 8 euros 50 each and says, 'Come on then,' and disappears into a door, comes back out and points at two booths.

"We were both very confused, but she ushers us into the booths and we've sat down, awaiting whatever delights our imaginations had in store for us. The reality was that the old bint from behind the counter started pulling her clobber off, which was *awfully* nasty. She looked like a bag of walnuts. I was obviously distressed and not looking at her so she was knocking on the glass wondering why. To this day I don't know what was going on in the booth next to me, but she turned her attentions that way, to my relief. I've never looked at walnuts the same way since."

PETE: "We were supposed to be alone in France but Alan turned up, or actually I think Alan came with us. He was drinking Long Island iced teas and taking Carl out to restaurants and to meet Mick Jagger. Him and Carl were out drinking every night and they met Jagger at some posh hotel bar. I didn't know anything about it. I was back at the hotel writing. There was no real time spent together because Alan was there the whole time, getting fucked up every night. That time spent there with Carl covered a certain amount of time, and then he went back to London and I was there on my own in Paris and things changed completely. I was struggling a bit and then all of a sudden I ended up with The Albion Rooms in Paris. Eventually it was like five-in-the-bed.

"We did the 'For Lovers' video, Douglas Hart [ex-Jesus and Mary Chain] came over to make it. I was enchanted by him, he's very spontaneous. I had fun in Paris once I got my head around the fact that Carl didn't want to be with me; he *was* very ill though. Everything and nothing, you know. He was just run down. At the end of it he came back to the hotel to find me and Douglas, Rene and Nadine, he was roaring drunk in a furious mood, a bit unhappy to see the place looking magical. He just started launching into this tyrannical tirade about how it was all over, he went, 'It's finished Pete, it's all over, it's gone now.' I said, 'What's happened? Has Gary and John quit?' and he snapped, 'No!' and I said, 'What, have *you* quit?' and he went, 'No!' so I said, 'Well, have *I* quit? Have *I* been chucked out?' He went, 'No, it's all over, it's Franz Ferdinand – they've captured the public's imagination, they're at number one, they've beaten us to it!' Me and Douglas were looking at each other thinking, 'What the fuck is he going on about?' – it was well weird.

"Things were as they've never been before. I was making a big effort to be with him, to show my love for him. All right, I wasn't squeaky clean, but I had nothing but love for him and I was trying fucking hard."

CARL: "I was just winding him up to try and get him with-the-plan. Which he was *some way from*, and if all he'd had in the first place was his own plan, he shouldn't have ever told me that we were sharing one.

"I had some severe family problems I had to return to England for, and then on my return to Paris, I was met by a lobby full of people from the internet and stuff so my plan had been scuppered. I weighed anchor and sailed back to Blighty."

With Carl back in London, Pete must have been getting bored because late one Monday night, he rang and invited me over there. "Come on, it'll be great. I've got these two Mexican schoolgirls staying in my hotel room, this French bird as well." I thought it sounded dubious when he added that the proprietor of the hotel was getting heavy with him over his unpaid bill ("he keeps *prodding* me") and could I come over and "sort him out". I made my excuses and said I'd see him when, or if, he ever got back to Blighty. I think in the end he played a set in the hotel bar to settle up.

The first of three sold-out nights at the Kentish Town Forum saw Kill City opening for The Libertines, with Doherty favourites, Chas'n'Dave, the unlikely main support. (Pete appeared in suit-tie-and-braces for their encore.)

PETE: "When you bring up *Top Of The Pops* or Chas'n'Dave, it's difficult to find the right words, knowing that they'll *all* do. It was wonderful, amazing, it was delicious, perfect, just-right. In off the underside of the bar. I'm not sexist but every lad knows how that feels. By the time they played with us at Brixton I was getting stuff in the post from them, invitations to go down to their gaff, communicating with one of their daughters and getting a bit of support as well. I don't think they dig my music actually. At first they pushed for a fee that they didn't get, they got taken down on their fee by Alan, who quite enjoyed sparring with them, but I don't think they really thought that they would be playing for Chas'n'Dave fans – they thought they were some kind of gimmick so when I got up with them and did a couple of the old-time numbers, they had me down as some sort of musical trainspotter, which I was when I was a bit younger."

Although the band had played a couple of trademark secret gigs since Pete's release, these were the first official outings to announce The Libertines were back. Each show was a celebratory affair, and coming just a week before Christmas they had a festive flavour, with Pete's old mate Jock Scot introducing them onstage one night done up as Santa Claus. Since Alan McGee had taken over the management, everything had gone up a gear and his enthusiasm permeated every aspect of the operation. For these shows, the Libertines merchandise, which up until then had been fairly mediocre, was spot on: a choice of T-shirts bearing Pete and Carl's faces in a Che Guevara-style iconic pose with the legends 'Free Pete' and 'Fuck 'em' respectively, black and white print on red. It was a step-up, more professional and the quality was reflected by their rapid sales.

The Libertines' set opened with Pete and Carl standing on Gary's drum riser with their backs to the crowd, the lights down and the crashing opening bars to 'Horrorshow' signalling the party was about to begin. Leaping down from the podium, ricocheting off each other the lights went up, the huge backdrop of the *Up The Bracket* cover was illuminated, and the place erupted. It really was something to see and I made sure I didn't miss a minute of all three shows.

TONY LINKIN: "It was brilliant to see them do that at the end of the year, and every night was different. It was going really well, everyone was really quite close. The drug thing was *there*, but it was more at bay somehow. The first night was just *so* entertaining."

CARL: "We did our best then, and I think there was some under-standing and I thought we were back on plan. Maybe we were. I don't know which part of Pete it is that decides that the minority plan is *the* plan, and not the plan and the dream that we shared. We thought we were back on track. From back on track to back on crack. That's why I'm always disappointed and seldom shocked."

PETE: "After prison I noticed that I started to feel a lot different before gigs, whereas before I'd be climbing the walls super-style, I can't emphasise enough what sort of torments Carl and I went through before going onstage – proper heebie-jeebies, running the gauntlet, everything turning inside out, and then all of a sudden it wasn't like that any more. Carl still had it. It's not nerves, it's the things we're about to go through and the things we're about to say and realising it was true. We'd have fevers before going on, but it became a lot less intense because I felt differently about myself and about my life after prison. I was making *absolutely sure* that there was only one reason I was where I was and that was because I *wanted* to be there. It hadn't been like that before. Not so much going-through-the-motions but doing it for the wrong reasons. I was really enjoying playing the guitar and really wanted to record the new album like now, now, now!

"The crowds we'd had before were a little bit more edgy, a bit more quirky, and reaching out to different sections of society. I'd say the crowds we were starting to get then were a little bit more main-stream, and a bit more homogenised."

In my opinion that first night was their best performance out of all three nights. They were all on form but by the third they were worn out, which was perfectly understandable. The opening show saw the band on fire, charged by electric nervous energy. Carl had seemed a little distracted when I'd run into him earlier. He later said that being in The Libertines you live five minutes at a time, and he didn't know what those three nights held in store until he took the stage. He needn't have worried. It was explosive, the two main protagonists re-discovering and harnessing that almost indefinable synergy, the rhythm section tighter than two coats of paint.

Between songs someone launched an apple stagewards and to my amazement, Pete caught it with one hand, took an aggressive bite, then smashed it to the ground before launching into 'The Boy Looked At Johnny'. It was quite a spectacle, cool as fuck and left me wondering how the clumsy character I knew pulled it off! Another highlight was the sight of Pete chucking his treasured Epiphone into the crowd where it was promptly set upon. I thought that's the last we'll be seeing of that, though amazingly his friend Chev (or should that be Chav?) somehow wrested it back.

At the soundcheck on the first night Alan McGee was waving the *NME*'s Christmas double-issue about with Pete and Carl dressed up as Tiny Tim-style urchins on the cover, straight out of *A Christmas Carol*.

TONY LINKIN: "Dressing bands up is always a horrible thing to do but it was the Christmas issue and it was kind of their year. They all got really into it, all loved doing it and as it was Christmas I just wanted to make it a real laugh. It was a weird interview because that night it was Carl who got really pissed whereas the previous *NME* feature it was Pete who got really out of it. They almost took it in turns [*laughs*]. I popped over to a pub with Pete and he promptly nicked a Union Jack off the wall; he was great fun to be with."

The interview within was typically madcap, Pete going off on all sorts of tangents, but my attention was drawn to a reference to Liam Gallagher. I'd encountered the Oasis singer at Lisa's friend Sadie Frost's house in Primrose Hill a few weeks earlier. We'd got on well, jamming on Beatles songs and having a laugh. I went to put 'Don't Look Back Into The Sun' on the hi-fi and, half-jokingly, Liam remarked, 'Get them fookin' burglars off the stereo.' It was all good-natured or so I thought, and I recounted the tale to Pete when I saw him the following day. It must have been still fresh in his mind, as later that day he'd shared it with the *NME* scribe and it turned up in the Xmas issue, though dressed up in a fashion that appeared a bit disrespectful towards Liam.

Alan advised me that his old charge might want a word with me or Pete, or both of us. I hadn't intended this anecdote to be for public consumption, but in a fit of characteristic irreverence Pete had blabbed it to a music paper and I was now being told that the volatile Oasis singer might be on my case. Of course Pete loved this mischief making and I couldn't stay cross with him for long – but then I never could.

The second night Gallagher turned up at the Forum with some goons in tow, somehow getting to the side of the stage during support act The Bandits' show. Security got rid of them, and luckily, I must have arrived just after they'd left. Whether Liam was there to kick off or just to see his mates The Bandits perform neither me nor Pete knew.

After a strange year, a sort of *annus horribilis* but with hit singles, The Libertines appeared to have a new sense of purpose. The Forum shows, a raucous Christmas party at The Rhythm Factory and the *NME* double-issue had seen relationships within the band return to something approaching normal. Pete had declared he'd not touched hard drugs for 32 days since his release from prison and wouldn't so long as Carl was around but something somewhere had gone wrong as I knew he was well into it once more. The cracks in the band's unity were merely papered over and this would once again prove divisive.

Pete's jail term and his subsequent reconciliation with The

Libertines put paid to Babyshambles and, along with it, 'Scarborough' Steve and Neil Thunders' aspirations of rock stardom.

Now Pete resurrected his side project, with an aim to record.

JAMES MULLORD (1234 RECORDS & BABYSHAMBLES MANAGER): "When we started doing [Babyshambles] it was always with a view to it being something Pete could do, bearing in mind his dislike for the whole 'industry' side of things and the disjointedness of The Libertines where you've got periods of intense activity to promote records and then long periods of inactivity.

"We were recording the first Babyshambles single, over Christmas to New Year 2004. Pete says, 'You've got to come all the way,' which basically meant I spent four days with him and he spent over three grand on crack and brown. It was a lot of fun but it ended in tears on New Year's Eve. That was the night it all broke down. But the four days leading up to it was just an introduction into Pete's world – snorting brown, piping, piping, piping and running around like complete fucking lunatics. I got home at about 6 a.m. on New Year's Day, took my clothes off and all my moles were bleeding, weeping blood. I was doing serious damage to my body I guess and I was fucking high, but I was smart enough to realise that I wanted to come down from that.

"I called Pete actually and said, 'Pete, there's rashes all over my body, my moles are bleeding, the whole fabric of the air is a matrix of stick insects, and the floor's covered in ants,' and he said, in his little voice of wonder, 'Yeah, that's how it is all the time for me,' and I realised how high Pete was at that time. He clearly wanted to show me where he was at, if we were going to work together. I just went with it. It was a good few days. I'd always had this relationship with Pete that was respectful but stand-offish; I was looking up to him and he was looking up to me but we really got down, got fucked up and brought those boundaries tumbling down [*laughs*].

"We went down to Rough Trade and I was sitting there with

Alan McGee who I'd never met before and Geoff Travis, and obviously I've a lot of respect for both those gentlemen. Pete sits down and says, 'I wanna release music with James – it's a matter of *honour*,' so they said, 'Well, if that's the case then yeah, all right.' He'd always said, 'I am going to release records with you,' and how he was going to invest money from his deal in my label, but of course he spunked every penny he got!"

PETE: "Approaching Christmas, after coming out of jail, always in my mind was Neil. I still considered 'Scarborough' Steve to be involved and to a certain extent that was the original Babyshambles, we were all in it at the deep end. One of the first sessions, I didn't really contact Steve, and just got Neil in and did a gig with Long Jim on drums. It was very strange having Babyshambles supporting The Libertines at the Duke of Clarence.

"Things were pretty natural. I *had* to have an outlet for my songs. The Libertines wasn't an outlet. I don't approach self-analysis or self-criticism with a false modesty. I do tend to genuinely doubt a lot of the exultation and commemoration we get, but now and again I will turn around and say, 'Yeah, I am a fucking brilliant songwriter,' and I'll put it into practice as well. I'll write songs and I'll be desperate for people to hear them, and love them and want to record them and release them. Carl is a lot less confident about his own ability sometimes, and also a lot more private about his ideas. For example he can't really be creative with other people there. He says that I'm the only one he can actually discuss ideas with. He often resents it when I write songs with other people, like *a lot*. And at that time I was starting to get things together with other people, simply because he wasn't there. He has his moments when he's really enthusiastic, really wants to get things done, but putting them into practice?"

The so-called guerrilla gigs that twelve months previously had proved such a bone of contention were now riotous and regular affairs, more often than not at The Rhythm Factory, with Carl back in the fold. The discord and destruction of the past year had done no harm to the band's profile, quite the opposite in fact, and now the bullshit had been stripped away, they were finally being judged on the music. The brilliance of those Xmas shows was followed by a sold-out trek round Glasgow, Manchester and Birmingham. Three nights at Brixton Academy would round off what the *NME* were describing as the band's "victory parade".

TONY LINKIN: "The tour was amazing. everything went amazingly well until the third night at Brixton. That night there was something about to happen. Pete was up for days on end, and that fucks with your brain anyway so you're hardly the most rational person. He turned up with some people and there was definitely an atmosphere. I've worked with bands who've done multiple nights before and the first night is always a bit dodgy, second night usually brilliant, and then it's a bit weird doing it a third night because you've already sort of done it all. Pete seemed more ill at ease on that night than he had on the whole tour, he seemed like a gun waiting to go off. I wasn't surprised when it happened.

"They finished 'Can't Stand Me Now', everyone left the stage and then came back on about 10 minutes later and started up without Pete. It's quite difficult to work out exactly what happened – he ran out into Brixton onto the street, no one could find him. I think he was wandering around Brixton, heard them come back onstage and then came back in again. The band were as surprised as the audience when he did wander back onstage, not that they didn't want him to reappear but they didn't have a fucking clue what was going to happen.

"After the gig I wandered in backstage and there was obviously a bit of a strange atmosphere. One thing I think Peter doesn't see sometimes is all he has to say is sorry to them and it would all be made up. He came back onstage and said, 'Sorry, I threw a bit of a wobbler,' or something to the crowd. Afterwards upstairs he just needed to say, 'Sorry I just lost it,' and it would have been fine probably. But he couldn't bring himself to say it, or maybe he didn't think he was wrong, I don't know."

ROGER SARGENT: "The first show, Birmingham, was pretty good and then Manchester the second show was out of this world and it just looked like they were gonna really fucking do it. The extra Brixton dates had just been added and we were like wow, they're gonna go global. Every time it happens, everyone involved still has this innate optimism that it's gonna be all right, and we almost put *all the bad shit* out of our minds, and then we get fucked up *again*! I'd heard a rumour on the second night at Brixton that Pete was going to split the band up onstage on the third night. He cut himself and smashed his guitar up instead."

PETE: "We were seeing scenes of adoration, but something didn't seem to click. There was definitely an estrangement, as always, before and after the gigs. There was unity in a lot of respects in that we were both striving . . . to go for it, as it was brand new to us playing places of that size. Alan really believed it, he'd say, 'You don't know how big you are,' and we didn't − it was a bit of an eye-opener. Perhaps it will annoy a few people but accolades like that, I dunno, I'm striving for myself rather than belonging to a group of people who have all that significance and importance. What I desire as a writer, or as an artist, is to stand alone and be seen as important and influential rather than be considered part of a group or part of a songwriting partnership. The songs have come from me and in a way I've been mugged of them.

"I was getting nothing from Carl at Brixton. I legged it up Brixton high street and realised I had no money and no drugs, they were all in my coat, and it was freezing cold so I had to go back. It happened during the second chorus of 'Can't Stand Me Now', Carl said they'd had a bit of a technical difficulty and they did 'Time For Heroes' and launched into 'The Good Old Days' by which time I'm back. I slashed my chest with a razor blade in the street and outside the door. I thought I'd liven things up a bit. I don't think most people knew what was going on to be honest. There was a bit of anger. Funnily enough, after that, walking up the stairs and sitting in the dressing room I felt closer to him, and the pair of us were happier than we'd been in a long time. There was a sense of finality almost. And absolute calm, amidst all that horror, and all the people who had been queueing up the night before to get in the dressing room and slap backs and pop corks and what-not, well there may as well have been fucking tumbleweed bowling down the corridors. Eventually one by one in they came but no one knew what to say, it was quite funny. And then there was the champagne laid out from the promoters – 'Congratulations!'

"I think for the first time in three days I'd really expressed myself. People recognise the foolishness, the childishness, the showy element to it, the attention-seeking element to it but they also see something, an expression, a pure expression. But this was nothing, cutting yourself was fucking nothing to what I was feeling; you could have slashed my throat and you wouldn't have done me more harm than what he did."

CARL: "He does that and then halfway down the street as he legs it into the night in some sort of dramatic show of God-knows-what, he hears on the security guard's radio that the band are still onstage and he legs it back on to get his glory. What can I say about that? We came offstage to find out what was going on. I didn't realise it was some pre-planned selfish act of stupidity. This is the kind of thing that time and time again breaks my heart and makes me wonder why I did any of it in the first place. Saying that I offended him during 'Can't Stand Me Now', it's just fucking paranoid . . . it's like me running out and saying I saw bats flying about the auditorium."

155

Shortly after this the Libs headed a bill at the Astoria in Charing Cross Road in aid of "Rock Against Racism" featuring The Buzzcocks and several other bands, most notably the Eighties Matchbox B-Line Disaster, who've got their own quite odd, individual thing going on. What a bill that was. Being a massive Buzzcocks fan I was always going on to Steve Diggle and Pete Shelley about how they must see The Libertines live. The two bands together on the same bill was like a dream for me, and as I filmed the 'cocks for Steve on his camcorder I spotted Pete bopping away at the side of the stage alongside that Buzzcocks fan and Libertines champion Morrissey. Likewise when the Libs took the stage I made sure Steve stood next to me and didn't miss a minute – not that he needed his arm twisting; he thought they were fucking great and realised why I'd been waxing superlatives about them for so long.

Watching The Libertines positively *on fire* that night with Steve Diggle and Mick Jones next to me, it really felt like, "It doesn't get much better than this." But it did! Mick breezed onto the stage (and no one "breezes on" like Mick Jones) for an encore that included a rendition of 'Should I Stay Or Should I Go?'. Pete and Carl pirouetted their way around the stage, doing backing vocals, while Jonesy held court in the middle, flailing away like, well, vintage Mick Jones! It was a pretty chaotic version – Pete and Carl bursting out of the traps a bar ahead of Mick, but the spirit was there. Afterwards there was a party at The Borderline but I didn't stick around for long. I just wanted to go home and preserve the night in my memory. I had to pinch myself the next morning.

PETE: "It was a special moment, me and Carl on 'Should I Stay Or Should I Go?' . . . Anyway it was Mick who was a bar behind us." [*laughs*]

CARL: "Yeah, that was good. We all enjoyed that, I think Pete had had some sleep. Mick forgot some of the words, bless him."

An appearance on the *Friday Night With Jonathan Ross* show helped to increase The Libertines' exposure as a bona-fide mainstream act. I knew Ross liked the band from listening to his Saturday morning radio show on Radio 2 where he'd regularly play even the more obscure album tracks, like 'The Boy Looked At Johnny'. He certainly pinned his colours to the mast, introducing the band as the best in the country, if not the world. They premiered 'Can't Stand Me Now' which I vaguely knew from live sets. It had clearly been written during those traumatic sessions shortly after Pete's release from prison, and the deeply personal lyrics left me with the ever-so-slightest of lumps in my throat. Pete's voice broke up as he sang, "You pushed me out and tried to blame it on the brown," but it was the line sung by Carl "light fingers through the dark" that did it for me.

PETE: "I wrote that in Whitechapel with Mark [Hammerton], well, he wrote a bit of it. Carl changed a few of the words around but it was already written to play to him when he heard it. On the demo of 'Can't Stand Me Now' it's just me singing it to myself but basically I got turned on I think by the idea of putting the words in his mouth, making them so personal, so he's singing them back to me. It was difficult on my part, not to sing the line, 'You twisted and tore our love apart.'"

Pete wore a skinny leather jacket over a bare chest which under closer inspection bore some worrying self-inflicted slash marks. When I'd visited him at his Whitechapel flat a few weeks earlier I noticed he'd done some DIY on his arms but dismissed it as attention seeking. Besides, the cuts weren't deep enough to warrant real concern. Pete's attempts struck me as a mild shock tactic rather than a genuine cry for help.

ROGER SARGENT: "I was helping Carl move house that day. Well, I say *helping*, it mainly involved me doing all the work while he rehearsed for the Jonathan Ross show! I get a call, 'Do you wanna come down?' so I went and it was really good fun, we were in the green room. McGee was having a drink – I was having loads of drinks. I was hammered by the end of it and desperate to get a camera off someone so I could do some shots. Sir John Hurt was there so I grabbed a camera off someone and ran into The Libertines dressing room and said to Pete and Carl, 'John Hurt's in there, let's do some shots,' to which Pete said, 'That's your thing Carl, you go and do it.' So we went back and John Hurt had disappeared so we had to settle for Shane Richie [*laughs*]. The band's performance was great, but very painful to watch."

CARL: "It was a good time, and it was new ground for us as well. And it's important for friends and in our relationship it's one of the catalysts, learning together, having adventures together. It was the first time we'd done that kind of TV show. John Hurt was always a bit of a hero of mine, but I didn't really speak to him, didn't want to. I've got very few heroes."

Shortly after this Pete popped up on the box again. Wolfman's 'For Lovers' had gatecrashed the Top 10 and he would be performing it on *Top Of The Pops*. Or would he? Pete had hijacked the song, which was essentially Wolfman's original, and while his vocal was infinitely better than Wolfie's, I felt that it was more than a tad unjust that the lupine one hadn't been invited to the *TOTP* studios to perform his own song. Pete had told me a week or so earlier that he wanted to perform the song as a duet with Wolfman, like two lovers serenading one another, but for whatever reason when the show aired there wasn't hide nor hair of Wolfie, just a suited-and-booted Pete fronting his backing band The Side Effects.

PETE: "Wolfman *insisted* I sing it; it was a gift, something very special. The same way Carl sings 'Boys In The Band'. It just came out, that vocal take, in the midst of absolute oblivion in South London long before it was released. It was *murder* trying to get Rough Trade to release that song. Murder. A lot of people have said [the production] is so bad, it's good. The backing singer, Frankie, sang on Marvin Gaye's 'What's Going On'. It's a ramshackle band but there is some quality there. Wolfman is a talented fella, you know, songs like 'Cyclops', 'The Delaney', 'Back From The Dead' they've all had input from Wolfman."

Rumours abounded as to why Wolfman wasn't present, they ranged from (a) he was deemed too scary for the young studio audience, (b) he wanted to keep his street credibility intact by not showing, to (c) he'd got lost on the *EastEnders* set which neighbours the *TOTP* studio. Though I felt the song was handicapped by a poor production job, the *TOTP* performance was a great if somewhat haunting one. Pete's eyes had a glacial, faraway look about them and when he raised his hands to take the mic his fingers were unmistakably nicotine stained and dirty. He was starting to resemble the Sid Vicious persona the press were likening him to. On the plus side, I remember noting that his barnet was back to its long and shaggy best. Typically, the following day he shaved it all off again.

JAMES ENDEACOTT: "We'd had that song 'For Lovers' kicking around for ages and we didn't want to do anything with it, it was a hit but we wanted Pete to focus on The Libertines. It just got to the point where we thought, 'Well, let's just put it out, let's just do it,' and it ended up being a big hit single. I went with him to *Top Of The Pops*, he had Dolly his nan there, he had his picture taken with her for the *TOTP* magazine. He was in a bad way. He was on the pipe quite a lot before going on. His mind was all over the place, he'd flit from one thing to another every five minutes – every now and again you'd get a glimmer of Pete but most of the time it wasn't him. He was a shadow of himself, it was quite sad really."

PETE: "I remember being in the dressing room at *Top Of The Pops* on my own with the minder Jeff, watching *The Man Who Would Be King* on DVD with Michael Caine – I gave my copy to Carl – totally enraptured. I remember saying to Jeff at the time, 'I wonder if this is how it's going to be from now on as a singer, on my own in green rooms.' I thought Carl might have come down, he was always encouraged, chased up like a bastard to come and play on that record and be part of it and he didn't want to. Then afterwards, I said, 'What did you think of it, "For Lovers"?' and he said that it lacked this, and there was too much of that and I went, 'Come on mate, it's not that bad,' and he said, 'You stupid idiot, come on man, you know I'm fucking jealous, aren't I?' I was dumbfounded, he'd never ever said that. Worldwide that single has been Rough Trade's biggest seller, it outsold 'Can't Stand Me Now' even if it didn't chart as high.

"The day I recorded it there was no other bands there, I think there was a bit of concern from the BBC who imagined carnage would ensue, so the Wolfman was banned for being too demonic. He made out like it was my fault and I didn't want him there. I remember getting a text saying, 'We're number four in the mid-week charts and I can't even score,' or something like that."

CARL: "I was asked for involvement myself, but I made at the time what I thought was a righteous decision to stay away from it because of the influences I knew were taking hold at the time. Need I speak the name? But in time no one noticed the reason I didn't do it, including Peter, and they got a Top 5 so I may as well have bloody done it [*laughs*]. Jealous? I wouldn't go that far. I thought it was a good song. The production? Yeah, another reason why I don't mind having missed it."

In early 2004, I promoted another secret Libertines gig in Camden. I broached the idea with Pete at noon on the Saturday, who affirmed

"Let's do it." I advertised on libertines.org in the afternoon, and a little over 24 hours later, we'd packed a mate's bar in Camden with over a hundred or so fans paying £10 admission. I weighed in Pete and Carl a tidy sum for what was essentially half an hour's work, and walked away with a nice bit of bunce for myself. The sound engineer was from the place where the band rehearsed and stored their equipment. He asked me to keep an eye on the microphones he was supplying. When I asked him why, he told me that whenever anything went missing from the rehearsal space the first place they'd look was The Libertines locker. I was exasperated. It seemed because of Pete's actions, the whole band were being branded as thieves, which couldn't be further from the truth. The fact of the matter is that a reputation like that can take a lifetime to shake. Who needs that shit?

The company Pete was keeping was causing concern, though. Every time I saw him he was shadowed by some geezer he'd met in jail. The guy seemed reasonable enough but an armed robber's an armed robber at the end of the day. I couldn't understand why Pete was now running with a different crowd. The more you'd try to reason with him, the more he seemed to thrive on the alienation and upset he was causing.

Having successfully put The Libertines on at a couple of different gigs for some quick cash, I was starting to entertain the idea of being a promoter. I was approached by an enterprising young photographer about getting the band to play a set at a photo exhibition he was planning at Filthy McNasty's. I came up with a novel idea to keep the numbers down and ensure the night ran smoothly. The first 150 fans to log on to his website could reserve a ticket at £15 each, which would also get them a photographic print of the band and ensure entry to the opening night of the exhibition. Of course we were inundated and could have sold the place out five times over. XFM were giving tickets away in a competition and I was quite proud of the way it all came together smoothly. We'd adorned the walls of Filthy's with 50 different prints of the band from this photographer's impressive and extensive archive and the place was packed with fans perusing his work, expectant of the acoustic set scheduled for 9:30.*

Pete arrived first, with Peter Perrett formerly of The Only Ones. It was a pleasure to meet the man who penned the new wave classic 'Another Girl, Another Planet', the intro of which I felt 'Don't Look Back Into The Sun' owed a heavy debt. Carl arrived with Alan McGee and I whisked them upstairs, where it was nice to see Pete and Carl greet each other with genuine warmth.

After they'd delivered a great set, myself, Carl and Roger Sargent headed into the West End for a late night tipple where we met up with Tim and Mark from The Charlatans. While Carl was becoming quite the pop star about town, receiving flash suits by John Richmond one week, being snapped by the legendary David Bailey the next, Pete unceremoniously slipped away into the night with his new friends.

---

* By the end of the night each and every print had been stripped from the walls by fans as souvenirs, as was the pub's sandwich-board, which I had quite artfully adorned with "TONITE: LIBERTINES SOLD OUT" in brightly coloured wet chalk. The exhibition was to run for a fortnight so replacements were hastily ordered.

CHAPTER 9

Oh My Friend, You Haven't Changed

JAMES ENDEACOTT: "Pete went into rehab three times during the recording of the second album, but within that and within the madness, he knew what he was doing. All Pete wants is his music to be out there which is why he uses the internet so much, and he knew that he wanted to do this Libertines record. He said, 'Me and Carl have been talking and if it's better than the first album we'll call it *The Libertines*; if it's not we'll call it something else.' He was out of his mind, doing a lot of drugs but he *knew what he was doing*. He just spent three weeks with them in the studio and then fucked off, but he'd done everything he had to do.

"Mick Jones was the only person who could have made that record, I wouldn't say he's a producer *per se*, he's a vibe man, he's really good at bringing the best out in people and they'd both grown to love him over the two years and he had a lot of respect for them. He didn't mind the madness because he could handle it."

PETE: "We've got this joke about Mick saying, 'Great,' quite a lot, and in the studio doing the new album, Mick said to Carl, 'It's great being here, isn't it?' to which Carl says, 'Yeah Mick, it's great.' So

Mick goes, 'Nah, it's really, really great. Don't you feel when you come in you're filled with a sense of . . .' And Carl goes '. . . *greatness*?' 'Exactly!'

"The second part of recording the album we moved into the bigger studio. It was very grand, very luxurious as well. There was another layer so I could sneak upstairs for a toot, and there was a big live room. There's no doubt about it. We wouldn't have stuck together and recorded another album if it hadn't been for Mick, it just wouldn't have happened, we wouldn't have pulled it together. I suppose I infuriated them [John, Gary and Carl] in a way. It definitely wasn't businesslike because we didn't really know what we were doing, either of us, we always had to be told what was going on. When Carl and I had a fight, Mick erupted. I might have misheard him but I'm pretty sure I heard him on the phone saying we were being pricks, maybe to his missus or something. He took me aside and said, 'It's just like me and Joe. You're brothers, you love each other, you love each other too much – you've gotta stick together, *stand together*!' I tried to explain to him that it was Carl, but it doesn't come out right when you try to explain it to somebody else, does it?

"I tried to explain to him that Carl wouldn't say the things he said to me if those fellas, the twins [hired security], hadn't been there to drag me off him. It wasn't my decision, I didn't choose to have them in there and I wouldn't have done had it been up to me. Alan would charge things to The Libertines but at no point did I sanction it, I just wouldn't have endorsed it. There was only one actual exchange of blows, but if that fella hadn't dragged me off [Carl] he'd have killed me, or I'd have killed him. He'd just moved into a new house and he wasn't in a particularly good mood. Looking back that was the crux of it, I think. That day we'd picked him up, me and my twin and we'd gone to Carl's to get him and his twin. He'd said, 'Quick, let's go before my sister gets back,' because his sister doesn't like me. I'd got this new recording device, and later on I said to

Carl, 'Why don't we set it up in your new house?' and he said, 'What's the fucking point, you're not allowed there anyway,' but in a really nasty, you're-not-welcome way basically. So I was like, 'Can't I speak to your sister and apologise maybe? Or maybe she can apologise to me?' and he just launches into it. 'Maybe if you sort your act out, clean up, blah blah blah,' and we start arguing, rowing, like shouting and that, no blows though. Someone says, 'What's going on?' and Carl goes, 'Oh, it's nothing, Pete just can't handle the brown.' I just flipped, standing on the glass table trying to go for him. I start belting him and in a flash he drags me off but doesn't realise I'm really going for it; I get out of his grasp and go for him again, full-on. He said it felt like a struggle to hold me off but to me it felt like I was Mowgli and he was Baloo.

"I don't think I was particularly excessive during that album. Occasionally I'd come in and just sleep. We really got stuck into 'The Man Who Would Be King', it changed shape so many times, also 'Cyclops'.

TONY LINKIN: "All in all there was three weeks of solid record-ing – they never worked weekends and Mick was having another child so it took a couple of months. Pete was great but he was really out of it. There was a near fight but that was over the usual drink and drugs thing; it was hardly *all* Pete."

CARL: "It was much harder, the time we did have we had to seize while Pete was *compos mentis*. I wouldn't have started drinking until dinner, about eight o'clock; only ever by late night, never ever in the day. There *were* good times, pure times, without Pete's ego or hidden agendas, without any of the history of what had been going on, without anything that was happening in the press. It was just musicians working together on songs and enjoying doing so for that very reason. There was no other agenda, and at those moments they were great times. Fleeting and far between but, nevertheless, we got our shit back. I wouldn't say better than the first album, but for those moments I won't forget that feeling, and that feeling is the whole reason I wanted to do this new album. I hope it's been worth it.

"There was bickering, graduating to Pete having a temper tantrum and trying to fly at me with an 18 stone security guard behind him. Mick's reaction? Sadness. I mean it's just boring. It was about 10 days recording spaced out over a month, and then Pete wasn't in for any of the mixing, or anything like that. It's preposterous really. He did turn up once or twice during the mixing period but all he did was sleep."

ROGER SARGENT: "I personally found it easier to be around than the making of the first album. We were waiting for a geezer to come down with some stuff and Pete and Carl were recording in the main room, and I'm in the control room. Somebody had a number for someone to come down and literally in the middle of the recording, like every *minute* Carl would stop and go [*agitatedly*], 'Have you got that number? I could really do with some coke, man!' and then Peter came up to the mic and said, 'Would someone get my *fucking* guitarist some cocaine?!?' [*laughs*]. It was quite jolly down there; I found the first album much more like hard work. Mick Jones was on fire, he was brilliant, dancing all the time."

GEOFF TRAVIS: "It was a pretty good experience for everybody, aside from the first day when there was a bit of a kerfuffle. Again, Peter was there the barest minimum time – it's a miracle he actually got down what he did. Credit to Carl, John and Gary, Bill and Mick, they were very hard at work. They crafted that record out of the scraps that Peter gave them. Then again there were other days when he was totally fine, and on fire and actually leading the band, orchestrating it. That was fantastic to see, and them playing together behind the studio glass was a sight to be seen."

With the new album in the bag, around about April or May 2004, the turmoil within the band started again. Where once they had been inseparable Pete and Carl were now leading individual lives that seemed sadly incompatible. I'd delighted at seeing them warmly greet each other at the photo exhibition, putting their differences aside to deliver a blistering set. A mere week later Pete's health and state of mind had disintegrated to the point where the tabloid vultures descended, milking him for quotes that were both damaging and upsetting for everyone involved, not least Carl. I was seeing a lot more of Carl than Pete and, sensitive soul that he is, he confided that The Libertines were all but over. He wrongly based these assumptions on what he was reading in the tabloids, begging the question: do these people care how they manhandle people's emotions?

It was around this time, when I was closely collaborating with Carl for this book that, with the band temporarily sidelined due to Pete's rehabilitation, Carl and his girlfriend Annalisa dreamed up the idea for a new club, Dirty Pretty Things, held at Infinity on Monday nights in London's West End. The objective was to create a scene where like-minded bands could play, presided over by a guest DJ. Over the next few months the likes of Tim Burgess, Har Mar Superstar and The Ordinary Boys appeared. I volunteered to DJ on the opening night, and on learning that Mick Jones had put his name down as well, I knew I was in good company. I began my set when a flood of young Libs fans began coming with requests. "Got any Libertines?" they asked. "Uh, no. Ask Carl, he might." I spun things like 'Velvet Goldmine' by David Bowie and The Beatles' 'I'm Happy Just To Dance With You' (from *A Hard Day's Night*) to the disdain of the young Libs fans that I put down to inexperience.

Feeling a lot older, I repaired upstairs where I saw John with his girlfriend Lena and his brother Rafe. It was the first time we'd met since he'd got wind of my book project and he asked how it was going. I guess the trauma of being in The Libertines has made John grow up fast because despite being the youngest band member he's probably the most well balanced of the lot – a long way from the impetuous adolescent I first rehearsed with. He wryly enquired how I could write a book without knowing "how the final chapter ends". I told him it's a work-in-progress and we shared a knowing, if somewhat weary, chuckle. Reassuringly, when he later took over from me on the decks, he cued up an original vinyl pressing of 'Old Brown Shoe' by The Beatles. Typical.

The night was going with a swing. It had been the hottest day of the summer, some 32 degrees, and inside the club it was a veritable sauna. Annalisa, with clipboard under her arm, was settling comfortably into the role of hostess and Carl was smiling for the first time in ages. Word began to spread that Pete was going to turn up, and, sure enough, he appeared in a straw trilby, skinny jeans and a rock'n'roll leather jacket, if not looking *well*, then certainly looking a damn sight better than the last time anyone had seen him. He had got out of rehab in Paris and was on his way to a tough detox camp in Thailand, but had 24 hours spare. It was an unexpected but welcome turn of events.

As the event was fairly low key, the crowd largely left Pete alone. I showed a nervy Carl downstairs for an emotional reunion. Pete had lambasted Carl in *The Sun* and said he was leaving the band but I knew it was some kind of tabloid exaggeration. While I couldn't confirm it was a stunt I strongly suspected it was merely a quick buck for Pete. With genuine affection Pete clasped Carl and mouthed in his ear, "You didn't believe all that bullshit in *The Sun*, did you?" to which Carl replied, "'Course not, Bilo." I found it a delicious irony that the tabloids had been duped, but I couldn't fathom why two close friends couldn't put their mind games behind them and just get on with it.

JAMES ENDEACOTT: "It was almost inevitable that the tabloids would pick up on it. When Alan McGee got involved, because Alan is a high profile figure, the press found out about Pete having a kid

The Libertines on stage at one of their numerous Rhythm Factory gigs,
5 December, 2003. *(Billy Easter)*

Mark Hammerton, who co-wrote 'Can't Stand Me Now', with the author and Pete,
Whitechapel, January 2004. *(Pete Welsh Collection)*

The Libertines at the *NME* awards with their award for Best UK Band,
12 February, 2004. *(Brian Rasic/Rex Features)*

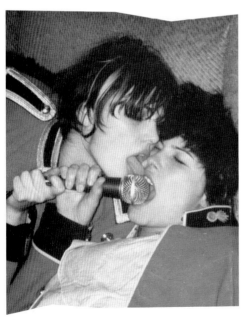

Mairead Nash and Tabitha Denholm,
AKA Queens of Noize, in full Libertine regalia.

Pete and Carl immortalised in ink, 2004.
(Nigel)

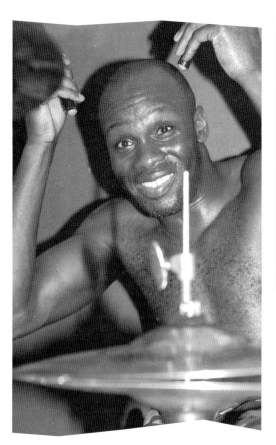

Carl considers a new career in Karaoke,
Soho, May 2004. *(Pete Welsh Collection)*

Gary, sticks aloft at the Rhythm Factory,
15 April, 2004. *(Emma Porter/LFI)*

Mick Jones with Carl at the inaugural *Mojo* Honours List,
London, 22 June, 2004. *(Ilpo Musto/LFI)*

Pete on Babyshambles business with guitarist Patrick, summer 2004.
(Pete Welsh Collection)

Pete leaving Thames Magistrates Court, 17 August, 2004.
(Andrew Kendall/www.andrewkendall.com)

Pete on stage in Babyshambles/minstrel mode, summer 2004.
(Pete Welsh Collection)

And then there were three: John, Gary and Carl in the EMI offices, Tokyo, August 2004.
(Pete Welsh Collection)

Pete on stage outside the Reading festival with Dot Alison, 27 August, 2004.
(Andrew Kendall/www.andrewkendall.com)

Arriving for sentencing for possession of an offensive weapon. Pete in high spirits
outside Thames Magistrates Court, London, 1 September, 2004.

(Julian Makey/Rex Features)

And backstage after a Babyshambles gig at the Scala in London, 6 October, 2004.

(Andrew Kendall/www.andrewkendall.com)

THE LIBERTINES

Carl onstage without Pete in NY, 12 October, 2004.
(Kristin Callahan/LFI)

with Lisa, and then Lisa and Liam, and just Alan's name suddenly made it more tabloid-worthy because they could mention Oasis. I read it, I don't like it and a lot of it's bullshit."

ROGER SARGENT: "I don't know how many nails in their coffin this band needs but that's certainly one of them. It's a sorry state of affairs."

CARL: "I don't read it. I've not even been in England. Occasionally people ring me and tell me and that. It's not about me, is it? Pete obviously wants that relationship with the tabloids, wants to perpetrate it, but it's not about me, it's about Pete's latest shenanigans."

Pete was more garrulous than I'd seen him in a long time and while the sparkle in his eyes wasn't quite there, he was encouragingly lucid, and apparently clean. He set up round after round of tequila slammers for me, Roger Sargent and the band's minder Jeff. Roger was shooting away with his camera when Pete commandeered it as he wanted to take a few snaps himself. As Pete whisked Roger's three grand camera off him, I jokingly remarked, "You're really sweating now eh, Rog?" to which he shot back, "Has he sold it yet?!" After the uncertainty of the last few months, it was great to see the band's inner sanctum lightening up at last. With each band member present, it wasn't long before all four took to the stage, using the other band's equipment to play a six-song set that fair raised the roof. I joked with John that the bass he was using was better suited to rowing a boat, but Pete had lucked out, playing a Pete Townshend-style Rickenbacker that I thought really suited him. I stood in the DJ booth for the duration of the show, watching a feverish crowd of around 100 go apeshit for this impromptu feast, catching Mick Jones' eye every now and then, bopping away unselfconsciously and punching the air in celebration. It really was a great night, and as the last chord resonated the crowd went into raptures as Pete and Carl embraced. With appropriate timing and the volume probably a little higher than the p.a. would have liked, I spun Primal Scream's exultant anthem 'Moving On Up' which seemed to capture the mood perfectly.

ROGER SARGENT: "While they were onstage, Carl said to Peter, 'You know you can't play with us until you're clean now, don't you?' and Pete pretty much promised that he would."

PETE: "I was the most sober person in there. I felt like I was the only one on that stage who was playing properly, with commitment and concentration and I felt detached from the rest of the band who were a bit sloppy to be honest. It's normally me thinking, 'Shit, Gary's bang-on and I'm not,' or whatever. I was straighter than I've ever been onstage, *ever*. I didn't think Gary or Carl were enjoying it – I didn't really consider John too much. I felt like a bit of a voyeur."

In true Libertines fashion, the surface celebratory spirit that prevailed at Infinity would not last long. The following day, Pete flew out to Thailand to enter a detox camp run by Buddhist monks, whose patron was, bizarrely, *EastEnders* actress June Brown (Dot Cotton). The patient was fed nothing but boiled rice and a thick, bilious elixir that guaranteed instant retching. A wallop with a bamboo rod from a hard-ass ex-marine was the punishment instantly meted out should anyone express distaste at the menu. After 30 days of this regime the case was made to sign a vow renouncing drug use, and sent home, clean but not necessarily cured.

Unsurprisingly, Pete sprung his way out after just three days. He thanked the monks but said he just wasn't ready for that kind of rigorous programme. Rumours abounded in the next few days that Pete had: (a) formed the Thai Libertines with a fellow inmate,

(b) gone busking in Bangkok, and (c) been shot. None were substantiated but the sad truth was they could all have been credible. It later transpired that he had paid his way round Bangkok by doing impromptu gigs at a radio station. Bizarrely, Thailand has a small but thriving music scene and was only too happy to accommodate a so-called British rock star.

PETE: "In Thailand I entered into this realm. It reminded me of certain times in my life when I've arrived in a new place completely alien, like moving to England when I was very, very young. I was cut off from my immediate surroundings in this room with 12 or 13 mattresses, bunks and lots of people who looked like they hadn't slept for a long time. No artificial medication, but I'd done turkey at The Priory anyway. They were expecting me to be a gibbering wreck. I was sleeping, and eating, I was all right – it was psychological. I couldn't stay in that place. I thought I was going to be isolated but I wasn't. I had monks coming up to me with photocopies of *The Sun*. There was so much confusion. They thought I was some millionaire rock star who was going to invest in the monastery. When I asked to leave I asked for my passport and money. All of a sudden the woman with the key couldn't be contacted, and mysteriously the phone lines were down. I started to get angry. I had a breakdown at one point. I said, 'Let me go.' They said, 'We don't think that's a good idea, the head monk is dying, he's very ill, it's a very bad time at the moment and you can't go without his permission.' I said, 'Look, I'm fucking English, man.' 'It doesn't matter, you've signed, you have to stay,' and I said, 'I wouldn't have signed it if I'd known that.' With the help of this bloke from Manchester I managed to get out but he was told by the head monk that if he goes to Bangkok and takes drugs, he'll die. He said, 'Fuck that.'"

Family, friends and fans were disappointed at Pete's failure to see through the programme, though to my mind, it was questionable as to whether it was a realistic regime for *him*. Within hours of returning to London, on June 17, Pete was promptly arrested for speeding offences, driving without a licence or insurance, and possessing an offensive weapon. It was almost a year since the burglary arrest and subsequent four-week bang-up, and when Lisa told me about this fresh charge at a Kill City rehearsal, I wondered where it was all going to end.

PETE: "I know Carl's got a thing about penknives, so I bought him one as a present. I was signing autographs in the station. They were a bit cold but they were reasonable, yeah. They know I'm an addict, it's quite well publicised, but it's the dealers they want, don't they?"

On his return to Britain, Pete entered The Priory – the infamous drying-out clinic for the wealthy, in Roehampton, South West London.

PETE: "It wasn't much fun but I went in for a particular reason and that's that really. The idea was also to get away from things for a bit, I thought, but it just wasn't the case – I wasn't getting away from anything. Yeah, Carl came down and brought me some QPR trunks and said, 'Come on, let's go swimming,' but the swimming pool was closed so he went home. It didn't really seem like Carl, he was with the bodyguard, and it just seemed a bit staged. I was told I was allowed no visitors and all of a sudden Carl comes in. I didn't want to see him, I wanted to fucking get clean, and do it and make him proud and that's the reason I was in there, for him, and then he came in and I just felt really dirty. He just came in and said how he'd been clean for so long, like three or four days or whatever, and kept going on about how much he was enjoying life and I just felt like shit – I don't even want to be in there."

CARL: "I did go and see him in The Priory. It was quite horrible really. I'd brought him a bunch of presents. I even got photographed outside QPR's ground with a QPR bag. Maybe it was just detached optimism but he was still kind of hinting that he didn't know why he was there."

PETE: "People in The Libertines' camp think I've wasted all this money and time on rehabilitation but it's not true; the time in the monastery, the time in The Priory were times of being clean, so it's not a waste, is it? You learn about your strengths and you learn about your weaknesses. Any effort you make . . . you can't knock someone just because they don't last the distance."

After a meeting with the band's management it was reported that The Libertines would continue without Pete Doherty, with the door closed until he remained completely drug free. *Q* magazine reported that Pete's bandmates and friends were "frustrated and desperate". Exiled and unrepentant, Pete embarked on a series of "My Drugs Hell" tabloid confessionals that practically made him, and by proxy, the band, overnight household names.

CARL: "Every decision I could possibly make in the wake of what's happened is shit, but I have to take one and the only guidance I've got which decision to take is what I believe to be right. I've said it as plainly as: if you stop doing that then we can be best mates, but if you keep doing that I won't see you."

I was starting to see more of Pete in the press than in the flesh so I was pleasantly surprised when he paid a visit to my mate's shop in the East End. This occurred immediately after Pete's Thai adventure, and subsequent arrest in Hackney. He cheerfully informed me that he'd kicked both his habits. I thought, "Stroll on son, you can't kid a kidder," and sure enough, moments later, he was in the toilet, heartily contradicting himself. Still, I noticed he'd put on a bit of weight, and when commenting on this, Pete invited me to have a feel of his biceps which he said he'd been working on. I gave them a squeeze, saying, "Go on then, tense 'em," to which he replied, "I am tensing 'em." A side effect of serious drug addiction must be delusions of physical might because he would have been hard-pressed to arm wrestle the bloke off the Mr. Muscle advert. I gave Pete a hug and although it was obvious the twin monkeys were still firmly on his back, as he pedalled off up the street it didn't really equate with the image of the oblivion-bound lost cause the tabloids were creating.

Pete had been accompanied by Mark Hammerton, once of The Senseless Things and now in The Lams. I was initially perplexed at this because word on the street had it that Hammerton was attempting to sue Pete for a cut of 'Can't Stand Me Now', claiming he wrote it. I guess, in their netherworld, grudges and gripes came and went.

When the single came out a few weeks later I was surprised to see the writing credit Doherty/Barat/Hammerton, as until now all Libertines releases had been credited solely to Pete and Carl. Furthermore, one of the bonus tracks, the reggae-tinged 'Cyclops' was billed as a Doherty/Wolfe composition. Now even Wolfman was getting a piece of Libertines action and I couldn't help thinking that this slackening of the traditional Doherty/Barat monopoly was another example of the once-tight partnership dissolving.

PETE: "If I could go back in time it wouldn't be that way. 'What A Waster' would be Doherty, 'Up The Bracket' would be Doherty. It breaks my heart to say it but after what's happened I think I'm entitled to abstain from crediting songs to someone who didn't write them, purely for the sake of mythology, when he himself has crushed to a fucking dust that friendship and that love."

174

CARL: "That's a very hurtful thing for me to hear. That's the reason we're not working together at the moment, I suppose. We've both had more input on different songs. I'm not going to get into a bitching fight about it but I don't see that as being true in the least – *in the least*. Maybe when he gets well he'll lose this 'I, me, mine' thing which he displays. That's something I don't want to be involved with; you can't share anything with that outlook on life. It just breaks my heart, saying after the event, 'Actually, that was mine.' I mean, *what the fuck is that about?* It's terrible. It really hurts."

The June 30 edition of *The Sun* showed Pete outside Thames Magistrates Court, suited and booted with a trilby, dancing a jig. "Prat In The Hat" read the headline. The paper's Victoria Newton reported on Pete's behaviour almost daily in her "Bizarre" column. When Pete offered her a confessional-style feature it was all tea and sympathy, but as soon as it became apparent that everything he'd said about cleaning up was patently untrue, the hack's pen again turned vitriolic, describing him as "Junkie Pete Doherty" and how he'd "bottled" the detox programme.

The broadsheets and music monthlies soon followed suit. "Annihilation beckons the dark star of rock", announced *The Observer*, with a photo of Doherty firing-up a mini Martell bottle, sitting awkwardly but poignantly alongside a band photo from two years earlier of him looking fresh-faced in his guard's jacket. One paper reported that Daniel Radcliffe, the kid who played the lead role in the Harry Potter films, was a big Libertines fan and had voiced his concern for his idol. It was getting to the point where I seriously thought I'd be seeing billboards advertising "Pete Doherty – The Opera".

Pete gave a typically frank interview to Garry Mulholland, under the banner headline: "I Don't Want To Turn Into Peter Libertine Rehab King", in the July 30 *Evening Standard*. With Doherty now officially an ex-Libertine, the article delivered the best write-up I'd seen about the current state of affairs and paid overdue attention to

Pete's aspirations for Babyshambles. With Pete proclaiming, "I'm not the sort of person who'll take a sub-standard alternative," Mulholland noted that Pete's guitar interplay with new boy Patrick Walden was "similar to the best of The Libertines."

PETE: "When I'm with the rest of The Libertines I tread quite lightly. They're very good at what they do and I appreciate it but I find Carl's quite rude with them, quite disrespectful. I think mainly the problem is, well, if there *were* more childish involvements and worrying about little things but there's just a general *killer silence*, a killer lack of communication. That would never happen in Babyshambles. It's a benign dictatorship. Nah, it's not even that really. It's all aboard the Albion, isn't it?

"I was pretty gutted the way the first Babyshambles single ['Babyshambles'] was handled, the fact that Rough Trade only released 4,000 copies when they know very well it could have sold ten times that. They sold a *lot less* records than they could have."

On August 25, Pete was mysteriously attacked near to where he was staying in Farringdon – being punched and kicked in the head and dragged onto the road where he was hit by a car. According to his press statement Pete only managed to escape by flagging down another car to come to his aid. Pete suffered cuts and bruises but did not need hospital treatment.

The September edition of *Q* screamed "Inside Britain's Most Dangerous Band" from its front cover. Not for the first time the analysis of Pete and Carl's estrangement focussed on the vastly different social circles the pair were moving in. Claims that Pete was disillusioned with Carl's admittance into the so-called 'Primrose Hill set' and that he'd lost his grip on the original ethos of The Libertines I found spurious, and just another example of the press trying to manufacture a more tabloid-friendly scenario. The point was whether scoffing canapés with Sting or slumming it in a Hackney squat, it was surely up to the individual. Neither are very good for you, but that's a personal choice. In truth Doherty and Barat had been going in opposite directions since The Libertines' formation.

If Pete did have a beef with Carl's new celebrity squares lifestyle, he'd have been apoplectic had he seen the August 2004 issue of *MOJO*, which showed Carl at the inaugural *MOJO* Awards rubbing shoulders with Sting, and Hank Marvin (of The Shadows) among others. He'd gone along with Mick Jones to present an award to Geoff Travis.

ROGER SARGENT: "At the *MOJO* photo-shoot I just remember Carl kind of sneaking in to the group shot. He wasn't meant to be in it but it's good that he was; he snuck in on the end next to Lemmy and Mick Jones. The photographer turned around to me and said, 'Who's that *cunt*?' " [*laughs*]

CARL: "It was like being in Madame Tussauds. It was a strange day. I was expecting a dusty little room like downstairs in The Poetry Café with a bunch of journalists, presenting Geoff Travis with an award. I hadn't had a great deal of sleep and then the taxi pulls up at Whitehall, the building where Charles I got his head chopped off, beautiful Rubens on the ceiling. John was there, Gary was there, I don't know *where* Pete was? [*laughs*]. They put me in the photo, and I felt like a right traitor and a right blagger, so I just knocked back the whisky, gave the camera a wink and thought, 'What the fuck am I doing here?' I just felt like a bit of an intruder. I'd have felt a lot more like a fish out of water if Mick hadn't been there with me.

"Then this over-keen P.A. guy came up and said, 'Lemmy says he'll meet you,' but I was trying to talk to someone and this guy was just pestering me. Eventually I go to the toilet with Lemmy and he pulls something out of his pocket and goes, 'Put that under yer tongue, it'll fucking destroy yer,' so I thought, 'Great, just what I need.' It was crystal meth and it certainly kept me going for the rest of the day. Sting was really nice, quite competitive, quite fatherly, told me I was too young to know about drugs. I just wanted to know about tantric wanks. Would it be called a tank?"

TONY LINKIN: "I never thought it would be curtains for The Libertines you know – they are the best. Pete will always be brilliant and make great music. Carl will be as well but when you put the two of them together that's where the magic is. I've always thought as friends they'll get back together, but it got to a point where everybody was like, 'We really don't care about the band any more, we care about you, Pete.' There was a point where he was looking like he might kill himself."

JAMES MULLORD (BABYSHAMBLES MANAGER): "Pat Walden will never be Carl, but this is a different thing – this band rocks, holds a groove, a proper heavy groove. We'd got to 32 in the charts with the single 'Babyshambles' back in March, it was fantastic. We only did 4,000 copies but we could have sold 18,000 of them at full price – that was the orders we got for it. We started doing a load of shows with little Peter and Jamie, sons of Peter Perrett from The Only Ones on guitar and bass. They didn't really fit properly, so Pat and Drew came in with Jemma on drums and that's gonna be the line-up. At first it was just different musicians supporting Pete to play his songs but now it's really gelled as a band. The transition happened at York; you'd always get chants of 'Peter' or 'Libertines' but when they left the stage there were 200 people chanting 'Babyshambles'. It was fucking brilliant."

MARK COLLINGS (FREELANCE JOURNALIST): "[Pete] came to Manchester to play at an obscure nightclub called Jabez

Clegg's. I didn't go because I was reluctant to fork out in case he didn't show, but there was one hell of a buzz in Manchester – it was like fucking Jim Morrison had come to town! Afterwards, people were saying it was great but they were talking about him like one of those classic rock'n'roller's from the Seventies, doomed to fuck himself up: part of the reason they were there was to watch the car crashing. What with the switchblade business, he was definitely becoming an anti-hero for the nation's youth."

PETE: "The gig that I played with Babyshambles in Manchester was the most extreme collection of hooligans and geezers that I've ever seen since I stood on the Shed at Chelsea when I was about 10. They were in a good mood though. I think they were attracted because it was a cheap venue, and it was a Saturday night. It was a self-aware Manchester crowd, girls as well singing, 'Oh Manchester is wonderful, it's full of tits, fanny and United, oh Manchester is wonderful.' I was scared until I realised they were having a good time. There was one lad who was really not very friendly. He was preaching really seriously 'Libertines! You've got to get back in The Libertines!' and trying to grab my mic."

A week earlier, I'd spent a rare day with Pete and had sat in on an impromptu Babyshambles recording session, and a photo-shoot for *Disorder* magazine. They must have amassed almost 20 brand new songs and the standard of the ones I heard was high, including a hard-hitting autobiographical diatribe called 'Pipey McGraw'. With a new band consisting of Pat Walden on guitar, who I'd known from years of knocking around Camden and Old Street, a lad called Drew on bass and a blonde chick Jemma on drums, they actually *looked great* also. Pete was as devil-may-care as ever and we had fun going out in the van to different East End locations with Micro Pete to take press shots. While I couldn't give Babyshambles my total, unreserved approval I had to admire the way Pete set about it. The

179

songs were pouring out of him and, in total contrast to the original haphazard Babyshambles line-up of a year earlier, the band were now looking a viable proposition.

A year had passed since Pete's imprisonment, and though in that time The Libertines had re-formed, toured to scenes of mass adulation and written and recorded the most eagerly awaited second album of recent times, history was repeating itself: Pete Doherty was once more out of the band, once more touting his new outfit, and once more facing a court appearance. Unlike the previous summer I felt Carl looked even unhappier and closer to breaking point; he was talking in private and public about some worrying "death threats" he'd received. Pete seemed unconcerned in making his private affairs public, openly feeding his addictions before disbelieving journalists' eyes.

PETE: "What I've heard from a few people is he [Carl] thinks he's made a mistake. He thinks he's made the wrong decision and he hasn't got the backbone to phone me and say, 'Come on, let's get on with it.' I don't respect someone who makes a decision, realises it's wrong, and then carries on. I don't respect that. I respect someone putting their hands up and saying, 'I was out of my mind on cocaine and whiskey, and I've made the wrong decision.' I wouldn't ever do it without him and that's that, I'm dead. It's unforgivable and there's no way back this time. I love the bloke, I wanna *live with him*, do you know what I mean? But it's too extreme, either way. I think Carl genuinely fucking can't stand me or he loves me too much . . . if that's the case he's gonna kill himself."

CARL: "There's a song which we both used to love which goes, 'If you choose that we will always lose, well then I'll sail this ship alone.' So you know, I'll sail this ship alone has been very appropriate. I don't fucking *want to*, though."

PETE: "I don't know what to say to people who think I'm gonna kill myself . . . *ahoy there?* I heed the words they say, but now my heart has gone astray, I've watched friendships slip away, anything's possible today. It's a game of two halves. At the end of the day if it's in the back of the net then I'll be chuffed for the lads, and over the moon, but I'll be sick as a parrot. Clucking like a bitch."

A Pete Doherty solo tour was organised with Dot Allison, who had sung on Massive Attack's records, providing support. The short jaunt around the country was a sell-out, but two eagerly awaited shows at Camden's Barfly and King's Cross Scala ended in confusion and disappointment. When I say ended, they never really started. The problems began when The Barfly's door staff stopped Pete's roadie Chev from gaining admission. In a show of solidarity Pete promptly left with him, leaving a crowd of 150 increasingly restless kids in the dark. You could almost see his point, though he should have just done the show and taken it up with the venue's management afterwards.

JAMES MULLORD: "It was totally ridiculous, a load of hoo-ha at the door with this bouncer getting a little bit excited. He wouldn't let in Chev and started pushing him, so Pete asked him to apologise which he wouldn't, so Pete walked off. He doesn't like aggressive or violent bouncers, and this guy was really unpleasant. That was the first bit of aggro on the whole tour. It had been fun, just general debauchery and a lot of good times, all in the back of a green transit van. Every 20 minutes I had to pull up on the motorway for someone to throw up because the pipe got the better of them [*laughs*]. It was crazy adoration from the fans, and pure riots."

The Evening Standard picked up where *The Sun* left off, running stories on consecutive nights with the straplines "Oh, For Pete's Sake" and "Doherty Doesn't Show . . . Again", referring to another no-show the following night at the Scala where Pete was meant to appear with Wolfman. The truth was, for the Scala show, Wolfman and his cronies had put Pete's name on the posters to guarantee a sell-out, but he'd never committed to turning up.

It seemed like there was nowhere for Pete to hide with *The Sun's* Bizarre column running a regular "Doherty Watch" piece, which couldn't have helped his precarious state of mind. The next time I saw him was at a Babyshambles recording session. With 'Can't Stand Me Now' entering the charts at number two (held off the top spot by the inane dance-dross of 'Baby Cakes' by 3 Of A Kind), and just about every publication on the news-stands reporting or speculating on his whereabouts, I found Pete stretched out in the back of a friend's Saab outside an unassuming recording studio on an industrial estate just off the Harrow Road. It was a hot day, stifling in fact, and apart from a profuse sweat, he was a picture of calm, listening to The Smiths' album *Strangeways Here We Come*, particularly ironic considering he was due in court the next day. Rather than quiz him about the serious business that was going down, I chose to tease him about my team Swansea's upcoming FA Cup tie with his boys, QPR.

Meanwhile, John had started writing and playing with his side-project Yeti as a creative outlet from The Libertines. His good friend Johnny Borrell's band Razorlight were rising through the ranks with their single 'Up All Night', bolstered by regular appearances on *Top Of The Pops*, *CD:UK* and a show-stopping performance on *Parkinson*, while Gary, who had toured with Eddy Grant before joining The Libertines, stepped in with minimum rehearsal to drum with the re-formed New York Dolls for two shows as part of Morrissey's Meltdown Festival at the Royal Festival Hall.

Carl was single-handedly tackling the job of promoting *The Libertines* in the music press and it was quite obvious the strain was showing. Previously Libertines' interviews featuring Carl *and* Pete made great reading – mad, fraught and entertaining – they'd bounce off each other like the best double acts. Now Carl was despondent, telling *Uncut*'s Craig McLean that touring without Pete was "one big shit sandwich and we've all got to take a bite." Maybe he had retained some sense of gallows humour after all.

CHAPTER 10

The Band Who Should Be King

*T*HE *Libertines* was a darker, more introspective beast than its predecessor, containing an all-pervading sense of paranoia that even jauntier numbers like 'Don't Be Shy' couldn't alleviate. Beguilingly claustrophobic in a similar (collapsed) vein to Iggy Pop's *The Idiot*, first listens to an advance promo copy left me drained. Though musically one of the more upbeat compositions, lyrically 'Can't Stand Me Now' set the tone for the rest of the album – the brutally exposed lyrics among the best they'd written. 'Arbeit Macht Frei' a 'Mayday'-esque blitzkrieg stomp with intelligent sentiments – "white kids talking like their black" – was pretty straightforward but Pete seemed to have a knack for making the banal sound incisive.

Standout track 'The Man Who Would Be King' was the older, more world-weary brother of 'Tell The King' from the debut album, and apparently Mick Jones' favourite. Another highlight was the seamless segueing of 'Narcissist' into 'The Ha Ha Wall', though listening to this most dysfunctional of bands fall apart before your very ears felt something of a guilty pleasure.

PETE: " 'The Ha Ha Wall' dates back to the very first night Carl and I, having met and having seen through maybe a year of animosity and standing-off, the first night we actually sat down as friends with guitars in about 1998 in Mortlake, above a furniture shop. We used to go down the all-night garage and he would start an argument with the fella and I would nick a load of firewood. We'd go back, get a fire going. He was really proud of his Union Jack tea towel and this old guitar he had, and the first song we wrote together became 'The Ha Ha Wall'."

The spirit of The Clash lurked at the start of 'The Saga'; Carl's uttering "high register operational" echoing Joe Strummer's "This is a public service announcement" call to arms on 'Know Your Rights' – the duelling, clanking guitars reinforcing the comparison.

It was frustrating to think it might be the last we'd hear from the band. Everything had revved up a gear; Pete and Carl's writing talents were indisputable, Mick Jones had done the songs justice and an instantly recognisable "Libertines-sound" was developing, but personally, for me one of the triumphs of the album was Carl's burgeoning guitar style. He seemed to play all his solos and lead-lines within a three or four note framework. It always sounded like he was threatening to break out and noodle, but he'd get the job done simply and effectively with a minimum of notes. Those angst-ridden and frustrated guitar lines seemed to sum him up, most notably on 'Last Post On The Bugle', 'Can't Stand Me Now', and 'Road To Ruin'.

If *The Libertines* was/is to be the band's premature parting shot, the closer 'What Became Of The Likely Lads?', described by Carl simply as "a testimonial", was just that. A damning, poignant lament to promise unfulfilled, and love lost. The hidden track, a lilting Carl-penned acoustic ballad 'France', suggested there was more than just 'Narcissist' or 'Vertigo'-style rockers to him, with a distinct nod to Davey Graham's 'Anji' lurking within the descending guitar line.

Press reaction was unanimous. "A masterpiece of life-changing rock'n'roll," Anthony Thornton gushed in the *NME* with a nine out of ten rating. *Uncut* conceded "The Real Deal" and awarded it five stars. *Record Collector* did likewise, announcing, "Amazingly, despite their troubles, Libertines trump debut album!" *Q* had an apocalyptic "Cockney rebels win the battle – Drugs may win the war" lead-line, and four stars.

Typically *The Sun*'s double-page extravaganza ahead of the album's release dissected each track with little regard for accuracy, claiming that 'Last Post On The Bugle' was the band's love letter to cocaine, and the noise on the intro was Pete or Carl sniffing a line. It was actually nothing more sinister than Pete ripping up pieces of paper.

At the same time as *The Libertines* was released on August 30 (though it had been leaked on the net a good month or so earlier), Pete announced a 15-date tour with Babyshambles for September/October, taking in many of the smaller venues he'd played on the 'Up The Bracket' tour exactly two years earlier. BBC6 Music would describe it as the nearest thing to a "Victorian travelling freakshow" – a definition its ringmaster would no doubt have enjoyed. After the furore surrounding the no-shows on his solo acoustic tour, Pete took advantage of Bobby Gillespie's personal invitation for Babyshambles to support Primal Scream's V Festival warm-up at the Shepherd's Bush Empire on August 19.

Opening with 'What Katie Did', the band acquitted themselves well if a little unremarkably. It lacked the sonic oomph of the Libs with Pete choosing to leave all the axe work to Pat but the songs stood up well. Primal Scream producer Brendan Lynch told me he preferred this incarnation of Babyshambles to the current Libertines and during the Primals' set, Bobby paid tribute to Pete and drew warm applause from the audience.

I hadn't seen Carl, John or Gary for some time but managed to catch up with Carl and John at the Reading leg of the Carling Festival on Saturday, August 28. Rumours that Pete was going to try and gatecrash The Libertines' set proved unfounded, though he did perform with Babyshambles at the nearby Fez club on the Friday night, returning to London before his former bandmates arrived the next day. Sandwiched between storming sets from bands-of-the-moment Razorlight and Franz Ferdinand, and a festival-stealing show from Morrissey, the lads were going to be up against it. They started gamely enough, romping through 'Don't Look Back Into The Sun' and 'Vertigo', though as the sun went down you couldn't help but feel that Carl was losing his grip on the tiller and the Albion was listing badly. While the songs stood up, they just weren't going over as they should have been. I caught up with John and Carl afterwards and they were chipper enough, playing table football in one of the backstage tents. It was the first time since Pete had gone AWOL that Carl seemed to be simply getting on with the job at hand.

GEOFF TRAVIS: "Imagine if they had played Reading with a fully functional band? They would have torn the whole place apart. It was all set up for them to be the kings."

On Wednesday, September 1, Pete Doherty had more pressing matters at Thames Magistrates Court. A later hearing time of 3 p.m. ensured it was a proper circus, with up to 100 or so rubberneckers present to see the accused arrive hanging out of the sun-roof of a car, guitar in hand crooning Oasis' "I'm free, to be whatever I, whatever I choose and I'll sing the blues if I want." No one could ever accuse him of not knowing how to make an entrance.

PETE: "It happened accidentally. In the end I had to take the guitar because I had nowhere to leave it, and I didn't expect that kind of reception. I didn't really relate my arrival to the outcome of the case. I don't think it would have influenced it. I was under the impression that the magistrate was going to rely on the probation report and my arrival wouldn't influence him. If anything I thought it might have helped my case, it would have shown my commitment to the cause, and that I was an entertainer and an individual. The magistrate wasn't that impressed by some of the gallery; it didn't really sink in with me how people were obviously concerned."

A host of witnesses offered character references including Pete's mum and Lisa Moorish, who said father and son were beginning to bond. A fan told of how Pete had performed a personal gig for his disabled daughter. District Judge Malcolm Read handed Doherty a four-month sentence suspended for 12 months, citing "exceptional circumstances" as the reason for the court's leniency. Claiming justice had been done and thanking everyone for "all the love", Pete skipped out of the court shortly after four to a waiting media scrum, and twelve months of (hopefully) good behaviour.

His first concern was in finding a new place to live as his short-lived tenure at a flat in Exmouth Market was, unsurprisingly, at an end.* Pete was threatening to come to stay with me for a week or so, which I okayed as we needed to spend time on this book and I'd do anything to help him out on the condition there were no junkie mates, dozy birds, and guerrilla gigs to contend with. A few days after his court appearance he turned up to recommence work on what you're reading now but I don't think he could stand the pace because, about six hours later, he thanked me and upped sticks into the night.

Around this time, *Q*'s annual awards nominations were announced on BBC6 Music, with Franz Ferdinand, fresh from bagging the Mercury Music Award, up for four gongs. The headline was "Franz Thrash Libs At *Q* Awards Nominations", with *Q* editor Paul Rees explaining on air that he thought the first Libertines album had been "poor", and though the new one was far better – the sound of a band "really doing it live" – they nevertheless weren't up for any

* A pity as it was a great flat above my favourite pizza restaurant in London.

awards as he felt the attendant "soap opera" had detracted from them. Maybe Carl's drunken outburst in that Paris hotel room had come back to haunt them, not that awards held any appeal for the band, certainly not in Pete's case. Speaking (ironically on BBC6 Music) a fortnight earlier, Carl echoed the sentiment that *The Libertines* should be seen simply as "a record" and not "two celebrities going through celebrity stuff", though he accepted that may well be the common perception. It seemed his fears had been realised.

In September, an open-air gig at Brick Lane's Vibe Bar saw Pete perform to perhaps his most eclectic audience yet, as part of the annual Asian Festival. A mix of locals, Hoxton trendies, Sunday shoppers and curious passers-by flooded into the forecourt where the stage was set up, and by 6 o'clock the area was completely packed. Pete performed an hour-long solo set, on a beautiful Gretsch guitar that I hadn't seen him play before, featuring a healthy smattering of Libertines favourites that a large number of swaying onlookers probably weren't familiar with. Most encouragingly, I could tell that Pete was straight as he pulled off some tricky harmonica lines while simultaneously strumming his guitar, something that would have surely gone horribly awry if he'd been on the hard stuff beforehand. It seemed like the few days at his mum's place might have straightened him out a bit. The following day's tabloids reported on Liam Gallagher's fury at "crack addict Pete Doherty's" failure to support his son by Lisa, with the tenuous claim that Liam felt the child maintenance he was paying for his child by Lisa was supporting Astile as well. The tabloid interest showed no signs of waning.

The following day I travelled to Paris to see The Libertines, who were midway through a three-week European tour (with Anthony Rossomando) to promote the album and to meet with Carl for another interview session. As soon as I stepped off the Eurostar I found two French music magazines *X-ROCK* and *Les Inrockuptibles* with The Libertines as cover stars. I bought the latter to find out where the gig was taking place, and inside was a cartoon of Carl and Pete, the former pissed rotten with cans and bottles all around him, the latter lying in a heap with needles hanging out of both arms. I couldn't translate what was in the speech bubbles but I got the gist of what the Gallic take on the band clearly was.

It was a peculiar gig; a small venue in Montmartre that barely held a few hundred. While the crowd gave the band a great reception, I couldn't help thinking that a Libertines line-up which included Pete would have packed out the considerably larger La Cigale Théâtre next door, and pondered if, without him, they could look forward to any real longevity. Carl seemed to be growing in confidence and enjoying it a lot more than at Reading, launching himself, bare-chested, into the crowd at the end of the show. Curiously the merchandise stall had no Pete-related T-shirts on sale, the "Free Pete" and "Likely Lads" tops with his mug on were nowhere to be seen. A few people commented on this and wondered whether they'd sold out, but I saw it as a cynical act of revisionism on the part of whoever took the decision.

As expected *The Libertines* entered the UK album chart at pole position, but with the band touring Europe and doing virtually no promotion back home, the record slipped to number eight, and then further to 16 the following week. For such a great record to burn brightly then die a death from lack of promotion seemed criminal. *The greatest album you never heard?*

It's now October 2004 nine months after Pete uttered those fateful words, "Why don't you write a book about us, Pete?" – an invitation I turned down at first as I didn't think there was enough to write about. Turns out I was wrong . . .

A few days ago the Babyshambles tour wound up with two triumphant performances at the King's Cross Scala on October 6, after a no-show at Aberdeen on September 29 resulted in a riot and seven arrests. The Libertines are a week into their US tour, and

'What Became Of The Likely Lads?' is to be released as the next single. The second Babyshambles single proper 'Killamangiro' is due out at the same time. Mick Jones has picked up a *Q* Award for his production of *The Libertines* and Pete is apparently considering an offer of £100,000 to appear in the next *Celebrity Big Brother* (wonder what his "one luxury item" to take in with him would be). Business as (un)usual.

What The Libertines' legacy will leave remains to be seen. I'd like to see them patch up their differences and get back together, but that seems a little fanciful at the time of writing. A third genre-spanning double album of *London Calling* proportions – their magnum opus if you like – is well within their grasp. If they can just keep from killing each other.

Equally likely is that it could all turn out to be for nothing. As I write I hear the thoroughly depressing news that Travis have been busted for doing a guerrilla gig. *Travis.*

It's enough to make you lose your faith in love and music . . .

GEOFF TRAVIS: "Maybe he's [Pete] rewriting the rule book [*laughs*]. Can you imagine if he goes on *Celebrity Big Brother*? It just seems like the most ludicrous thing ever. Most people who are in that position have got really minor talent. Hank Williams got married onstage and charged people money. I can see Pete doing that."

CARL: "I don't know what the future holds any more, it's quite scary. I've got some kind of faith in optimism. I hope that friendship will out, above all else. Even if we never play again together, that would be nice. There's something in me and Peter which is true friendship. I don't know how much of that gets lost, it's just a matter of caring about it enough to bring it out. What do they say, time's a great healer? Absence makes the heart grow fonder? But then they also say, out of sight, out of mind.

"I've known a lot, I've grown a lot and these last few years all I've known is what's been my life, so I wouldn't change it . . . I mean, well, obviously I'd change a *few* things [*laughs*]. I'd like to think it's all happened for a reason."

PETE: "Things aren't exactly perfect so maybe I'm painting a picture of doom and gloom but God forbid that I would want to detract from the amazing times we had, round the piano with Mick, round the piano with John and Gary."

POSTSCRIPT

Possibly the best barometer of where Pete and Carl's individual and collective fortunes lay came with the simultaneous release of Babyshambles' 'Killamangiro' and The Libertines' 'What Became Of The Likely Lads' in November 2004. Pete's anti-hero public image seemed to have helped relegate his former band to playing second fiddle to Babyshambles new, more angular and exciting sound. That 'Killamangiro' was a fresh and fantastic single was indisputable, and it received blanket coverage on xfm and MTV2, but 'Likely Lads' seemed to sink without trace. With little or no promotion it performed poorly in the charts and was a sad afterthought to The Libertines' story. It was a story in which the music had become a mere sideshow to Pete's increasingly erratic antics, and the next six months would see his profile and notoriety go through the roof.

Despite an encouraging tour of the States, including a big splashdown in Hollywood where the stars came out to see them, in early November Carl announced that The Libertines would be splitting at the end of the year. The inevitable could not be delayed any longer, though typically magnanimously Carl paid tribute to his erstwhile partner and expressed his hope for a reconciliation some time soon. That looked increasingly doubtful given Pete's behaviour with Babyshambles, which saw him wreck a valuable piece of modern artwork during a riotous set at the Groucho Club in Soho of all places. The tabloids had a field day. One of many that would follow.

Far from resting on his laurels, Carl busied himself lending guest vocals to Client's 'Pornography' single, an electro-pop tune which was quite a departure from his usual fare, and showcased his well-heeled English vocal styling. *NME* also reported on a new 'supergroup' he'd light-heartedly put together with Tim Burgess, Duffy from Primal Scream, and the drummer out of Razorlight, for a one-off gig at the Tap'n'Tin, the Chatham venue that had hosted The Libertines' reunion gig after Pete's jail sentence.

If Carl was dutifully getting on with things, the same could definitely not be said of Pete, who would embark on one of his maddest weeks ever, even by his (high) standards. With a fortnight to go to Christmas, a scheduled appearance on *Top Of The Pops* ended, perhaps predictably, in total chaos. Pete leapt from the stage during a performance of 'Killamangiro' and set about an audience member for reasons unbeknown to anyone, a mass brawl ensued and the BBC had to broadcast a rehearsal take. Worse was to follow on Babyshambles' biggest tour to date, taking in sizeable venues in Blackpool, London, Belfast, Dublin and Glasgow. In Blackpool Pete was reported to have "gone mad", being barely able to stand let alone perform on stage. Understandably, though, for the first time the paying public weren't having it, booing and throwing bottles, various members stormed off stage, and an incoherent, confused Pete was forcibly pulled off. His reaction was to perilously climb the speakers and launch himself into the heaving mass of fans, who ripped his top off in a frenzy.

The circus returned to town for an eagerly anticipated show at London's Astoria. I sat in the band's dressing room, tucking into the rider awaiting Pete's arrival. When, at 2.15 in the morning he hadn't shown and it was announced to 2,000 restless and frustrated fans that the show was off, a full-scale riot broke out, with the stage trashed and equipment stolen or destroyed. I stayed upstairs but the racket was quite something, with police vans on the scene pretty sharpish. Within hours a guitar pedal pilfered from the stage appeared on eBay! Rumour had it that Pete had arrived at the venue, alone in a taxi, then promptly scarpered down Tottenham Court Road, though why no one knows.

The day before the Astoria no-show, Carl had officially wrapped up Libertines business at the 287 Club in Paris, supporting PJ Harvey. In stark contrast to the attention afforded to Pete's shenanigans, his former band's demise went largely unreported. There was no let-up in the media clamour for Pete Doherty though, with a 20-minute grilling from Kirsty Wark on BBC2's worthy *Newsnight* show, a setting usually reserved for politicians and the like. After a Christmas spent with his parents, Pete embarked on an ambitious four-gigs-in-a-night tour for New Year's Eve, taking in Birmingham, Stoke, Oldham and Manchester. Considering he couldn't get it together to do a show in his own backyard, this seemed an unlikely prospect, though amazingly he pulled it off, the first show commencing at 8 p.m. and the last at 3.15 a.m. in the New Year. The scenes of mass adoration prompted *NME* to declare it "Peatlemania"!

Things seemed to go from bad to worse for Carl though. He'd hinted at some kind of health problem towards the end of The Libertines and in early January revealed he would be having a tumour removed from behind his ear. I know that in private he was pretty scared and who can blame him, but in public he manfully kept his chin up, telling *NME* that he was optimistic for the future, having had some sense of closure on the Libs, and how he admired and rated John Hassall's efforts with his new band Yeti. John's Beatles-influenced outfit would chart in March with debut release 'Don't Ever Lose Your Sense Of Wonder' and garner much praise from Noel Gallagher amongst others.

Nothing runs smoothly in Pete's world, though, with his drummer Gemma Clarke quitting Babyshambles in late January, citing her problems with the band's management as the reason for her leaving. A new fella called Adam Ficek was drafted in at short notice, and made his debut at a tsunami benefit at the Garage organised by Danny Goffey and Rhys Ifans, the hellraising Welsh actor. Putting Pete and Rhys together is like mixing Stella with Strongbow, as I know from vast personal experience of both. They hit it off straight away, and Pete delivered a blistering set. The event was a media circus, with paparazzi everywhere. They certainly got the result they wanted, as the following days tabloids were full of it, with a photo of a sweat-drenched Pete with his eyes rolled back, showing only the whites, looking properly zombied-up and hurling himself into the crowd. "Night of the Living Dead" screamed one, and the general tone seemed to question whether this "junkie rocker" was a suitable role model for the nation's youth. Whatever, this was nothing compared to the madness that was to unfold in the coming week, which must rank as the most extreme in the life and times of Pete Doherty.

A burgeoning relationship with model Kate Moss – nobody really knew if it was credible or not – ensured Pete was front-page tabloid news more or less every other day for a week or two. Pete, who had chastised Carl previously for hanging out with the faces in Primrose Hill, had evidently launched himself into that very world with his dalliance with Kate. I wasn't at all surprised she had fallen for him though, he's a very charming fella, but she must have insisted that he wash his hands which are infamously dirtier than a miner's. Pete was gleefully telling the world of their "true love" in his most candid interview ever in the *Mirror*, talking about his family, his music, drugs, and he and Wolfman cutting each other up and rolling around in their blood. *Nice.*

No sooner had these revelations been digested by an increasingly disbelieving public than the news broke that Pete had been arrested on suspicion of assault and robbery. It unfolded that there'd been an incident at a hotel in Clerkenwell where a filmmaker called Max Carlish had been beaten up. I'd met this fella once as he was following Pete around to make a documentary. He admitted selling stills of Pete smoking smack to the *Sunday Mirror*. Pete and a goonish sidekick had met up with Carlish in this hotel, and one way or another he had emerged with a hell of a shiner. Typically the whole affair was shrouded in mystery, but, whatever did happen, Pete was getting his collar felt pretty soon after the infamous February 2 incident. Apparently the old bill couldn't interview him for some 15 hours after his arrest as a police doctor examined him and said he was high on "all sorts of drugs" – and even showed evidence of injecting in his hands. Again – *nice*.

Pete's victim seemed to revel in the frenzy of attention and media coverage, but confusingly claimed he wanted the charges – which were by now of robbery and blackmail – dropped. It was to be a pretty shitty weekend for Pete, who ended up banged up in Pentonville Prison (ironically on the "Cally Road" he sang about on 'Up The Bracket') for six days whilst James Mullord mustered up the £150,000 needed to bail him out. The press interest was relentless, Pete giving an exclusive to *The Sun* on his release, describing his incarceration as "hell on earth" and revealing he was straight off to rehab and a naltrexone implant to fight the heroin addiction.

One of the conditions of his bail was a 10 p.m. curfew with a date in April set for his hearing. Pete found himself facing the very real prospect of doing four year's bird, even though the charges were thought by Pete to be nonsensical. He seemed nonplussed at the grave nature of his fate, and got back on stage as soon as he could, doing a 35-minute set back at the Garage on February 21, at 8.50 so he could get home and tucked up in bed as ordered by the judge.

The Garage show was a warm-up for Babyshambles' biggest gig yet, in front of over 4,000 fans at Brixton Academy. If anything, the mood was even more exultant than at the three-night stand he'd played with The Libertines almost exactly a year earlier at the very same venue. It seemed he couldn't put a foot wrong and the show was outstanding, apart from a vicious brawl with guitarist Pat that held up proceedings for 10 minutes. There had been trouble earlier when Pete cut short 'The Man Who Came To Stay' to order everyone back as people were getting dangerously crushed at the front.

Yet more controversy beckoned when, bizarrely, the leader of the Conservative Party, Michael Howard, got in on the act, raising Pete's name in the Commons: "Here you have a man who takes drugs and gets locked up yet ends up on the front pages," and how he was "making drug-taking cool". Far be it from me to agree with a Tory but you can't really argue with that, can you?

Pete did his public image no favours with an appearance on ITV's *Orange Playlist*, a picture of wasted druggy-chic, selecting his favourite songs and chatting with Lauren Laverne. I was pleased that in among The Specials and Kings Of Leon he chose to push The Paddingtons as his tip for the top. I'd just returned from a 10-date tour supporting The Paddingtons and they are a cracking bunch of lads from Hull. More than any other new band they are probably the first to have been truly influenced by Pete and The Libertines, and they don't mind admitting it. I know that when Pete plugged them on the box they were chuffed, and so was I for them.

Fortunately an appeal to extend Pete's bail conditions to allow him to go to Wales to start work on Babyshambles' debut album fell on kind ears and by the end of March 12 songs were recorded in seven days at the remote Twin Peaks Studio with Mick Jones at the helm. Naturally reports emerged of the place being trashed and eventually the band were asked to leave for not falling in with the hippy, new-age ethos of the establishment. Still, early reports suggest the album is a corker.

And so to the end. Chaos still reigns in the kingdom of The Libertines and Pete Doherty but as we enter the summer, whisper it quietly, but things may just be looking up. April has seen all charges against Pete dropped and even more encouragingly he and Carl have met and been reconciled; a chance meeting in the Boogaloo Bar in Highgate saw them greet each other warmly if a little nervously for the first time in nearly a year. Babyshambles' album is almost in the bag, and Carl can boast a £1 million solo record deal. Whatever they do individually, in my opinion there's no question that The Libertines will be back, all four of them, on a stage in the future. A Pistols-style megabucks reunion. Can you imagine? A time for heroes . . .

09/05 (56110)
456789